Boozy Food

Tony Lord
with
Jill Cox

HEADLINE

*With special thanks to Dianne Curtin
for her invaluable help.*

First published in 1994
by HEADLINE BOOK PUBLISHING

10 9 8 7 6 5 4 3 2 1

ISBN 0 7472 4654 8

Typeset by
Letterpart Limited, Reigate, Surrey

Printed and bound in Great Britain by
Cox & Wyman Ltd, Reading, Berks.

HEADLINE BOOK PUBLISHING
A division of Hodder Headline PLC
338 Euston Road
London NW1 3BH

CONTENTS

INTRODUCTION

I arrived in London just before Christmas in 1969. My Australian friend Andy, who was travelling with me, accepted an invitation to a Christmas party in the country, but I opted to stay in London to have lunch with some Antipodean friends.

I will never forget walking down Baker Street, not a soul in sight, with a bitter wind whipping up old newspapers. It was a scene straight out of the film *On the Beach*. Matters were not helped by knowing that back home my family and friends were drinking champagne around the pool.

Shortly afterwards, Andy and I rented a flat. Andy was a useful person to travel with as he is rather large and strong, and I think a few people decided not to take a swing at me when they had a look at him. However it quickly became apparent that boiling an egg would be a challenge to him, so I had better learn to cook.

I had never had to cook at home, so this was a new experience for me. As we were well near broke we could not afford to eat out, nor could I just buy a steak or two, because by Australian standards a decent steak in London was, and still is, frightfully expensive.

So I started to play with stews and spaghettis, and was rather amazed to find that while sitting in the kitchen at home watching my mother cook dinner, I had subconsciously absorbed what had to be done and how to do it.

I found I enjoyed cooking. If you do, it can be quite

1

relaxing. Gradually I collected recipes from various sources and became more adventurous. I then got a job on a wine magazine and the odd cook book review copy began to surface. I also began to travel to different wine-producing countries. Of one thing you can be certain: if you are in a vineyard area, you are going to find fine food as well. Wine producers take more than a passing interest in matching their wines with fine foods.

I discovered the delights of eating in Paris. In Australia, the cuisine in my youth was totally dominated by British culinary conventions to the extent that while the temperature might, and often did, soar to 105° F on Christmas Day, one still had to sit down to a piping hot roast turkey.

In Perth, where I lived, there was one Italian restaurant, and it was a pretty adventurous thing to eat there. I later realised that the only thing Italian about it was the owners. The food was very non-Italian, and everyone drank beer.

So French food was a revelation. I then discovered Italian food was different from French, and Spanish from Italian. In passing I might say that while I have a deep affection for the cooking of Tuscany, to me the finest country in the world to eat in is Spain. Each region has its own traditions and specialities, and the Spanish do not treat their food with the pomposity I have encountered in France.

As I moved around I picked up all sorts of bits and pieces that I added to my culinary baggage. For example in Australia, everyone cooked with lard. Outside the Italian community, no one had ever heard of olive oil. Or that off the coast we had huge shoals of sardines which everyone netted for bait. No one actually thought of eating them.

With a colleague I went on to found my own wine magazine, and travel even further abroad.

In downtown San Francisco I discovered the best chopped steak sandwich in the world, and the China Moon Café, where there is some of the most inventive Chinese cooking I have ever come across. In Cape Town I ate a stew made with the flowers of water lilies. In Adelaide, I had my first taste of kangaroo meat, which had just been legalised for human consumption, though out in the bush they had been eating it for years. I found the meat was rather too gamey for my taste, but as I was with Max Schubert, the creator of the legendary wine Grange Hermitage, who had brought a bottle along with him, who cared.

In Hong Kong I tried bird's nest soup, though I avoided live monkey brains, and in the Singapore markets watched a live bat being despatched for a lady's lunch. In Spain I had a dish, quite delicious, that I thought was a stew made from local beans. It turned out that the beans were, in fact, roosters' testicles. It was fairly quiet in the morning in that part of the world. On returning to Australia after a long stretch in London, I found that not only was kangaroo available, but so was crocodile, water buffalo, emu, feral goat and others. At last some use had been found for what were previously considered pests. Also local chefs were finding exciting uses for roots, plants, fruits and barks that the Aboriginals had long used as a food source. These experiences were fascinating, and brought home quite forcibly the point that what some people will not eat, others will.

They also developed my tastes to the point where I now know what I really like, and what I do not. Italian, Spanish and Chinese are my favourite cuisines, but I have found it hard to come to grips with many aspects of Japanese food.

This was not so much a gastronomic voyage of discovery, but a gastronomic awakening. I hope if you are just learning to cook, or already are honing your skills, you will have the same experience.

BOOZE AND FOOD

Alcohol, and in particular wine, has been a part of civilisation and its gastronomy for thousands of years. The word alcohol is itself Arabic, and comes from the words *al khol*, the black powder made using distilled spirit, and which is widely used, even today, as an eye cosmetic.

The first alcohol was wine. The first vines are thought to have originated in what is now part of Iran, and their cultivation became widespread throughout the Middle East. The Roman historian Pliny described large vineyards in Palestine, and Lebanon was a famous producer. It still is today.

One can only speculate that the first wine was made when someone left some grapes that were damaged in a jar. The juices fermented and the owner found he had a pleasant drink.

Wine had many uses in ancient society. It was drunk as a beverage by many, though not the Persians. The cautious Hebrews mixed it with water, a heinous practice that history attributes to Cranaus, King of Athens, in 1532 BC. In Egypt and elsewhere it was used in religious ceremonies, and the Phoenicians traded widely throughout the Mediterranean in wine. It was even infused with herbs and other ingredients as a medicine.

The vine reached Europe via the Greek islands and Greece. The Ancient Greeks took to wine with a vengeance. There are constant references to wine in the writings of Homer, it being offered to the Gods, and enjoyed in excess by mortal men. He even uses it in epithets like "the wine-dark sea". The Greeks got a bit picky about their wine, with the rosé wine of Chios being much favoured.

The Greeks passed the baton to the Romans who proved even more enthusiastic about the product of the grape, holding two wine festivals: the first in May celebrated the first taste of the new wine, and the second in September was to offer prayers to the god Jupiter for an abundant harvest. They also regularly sung the praises of the wine god Bacchus to the extent that the word 'bacchanalian' has passed into the language to describe an orgy of food and drink.

In various writings by Romans like Pliny, it was clear that some of the modern wine-making practices were already in use. They cleared the wine of fine solids using egg whites, which is still done today. They also knew that if a wine was left in a wooden cask for three or four years, it improved immeasurably. You could also say they were into vineyard selection, because Roman connoisseurs knew that the best Greek wines came from Lesbos, Chios and Cos, and their own best wines from Falernum, Albanum and Mamertinum.

The Romans and the Greeks both used to flavour wines. The Greek retsina flavoured with pine resin has its origins in this practice. The Romans, however, found it a convenient way to disguise bad wine. The Roman gourmand Apicius mentions several popular flavoured wines, with *rosatum* (rose petals), *granatum* (pomegranates), *mulsum* (honey) and *violatum* (violets). Vermouth and pastis are descendants of these drinks.

It must be said that the early Romans were chauvinists when it came to wine. Women were not allowed to drink

it, and one Micennius burnt his wife to death on the cask
on which he found her helping herself. But, by the time
of Caesar, the girls had been let in on the party, and
Livia, the consort of Augustus, claimed she lived to the
ripe old age of eighty-seven, which was pretty amazing
in those days, thanks to Bacchus and his friends.

With the march of the Roman legions the vine spread
into Europe: Spain, France, England, Germany, and the
modern Yugoslavia. There a Roman emperor ordered
the vines pulled out, and his legionnaires responded by
putting him to the sword.

The culture of the vine and wine drinking had become
pan-European by the time of the Emperor Charlemagne,
and wine was not only used as a beverage, but also in
religious ceremonies, as presents, and for paying fees.

It is uncertain when wine was first used in the preparation of certain foods, but most likely it was introduced by
the Greeks. It was certainly established by Roman times
when such delicacies as pheasant sausages made with
pheasant, pepper, gravy and sweet wine were served at
banquets.

While the early Europeans drank wine, elsewhere in
the world the main form of alcoholic beverage was a
primitive form of beer. In the Africas it was, and still is,
made from mealie maize, while in the Americas it was
made from corn. The Aztecs had a drink, widely used
ceremonially, called *chicha*; they are said to have started
the fermentation by spitting into it. I have tasted *chicha* in
Peru, and it was rather like thick raspberry cordial. I did
not ask how they fermented it.

The art of distillation also has a long record. It was
thought to have been discovered in Mesopotamia around
3500 BC, where it was used to make perfumes and
essences. The Chinese are also said to have used it around

800 BC to make a spirit called *alaki* from rice beer, possibly the first evidence of the distilling of alcohol.

The Arabs perfected the art of distillation. Their religion forbade the drinking of alcohol, but they used it for medical and scientific purposes. As the Egyptians had already discovered, alcohol was an ideal medium in which to infuse or macerate herbs and other ingredients to create perfumes and potions.

Through the Moorish conquests of southern Spain, the Arabs passed the knowledge of sophisticated distillation into Europe. The art was certainly well enough known by the 1100s. At first it was mainly confined to centres of learning, and in particular monasteries, where spirits were used as a base for medicines, in which many liqueurs had their origin. Chartreuse is a classic example, having been used to combat an outbreak of cholera.

As the knowledge spread, alchemists saw distillation as a way of transmuting base metals into gold. Nothing came of that, but gradually other uses, including drinking it, were found for the resulting spirits. The classic French brandy, Armagnac, was already in commercial production by 1411, and Alsace and northern Italy were also distilling centres.

Spirits began to enter the gastronomic world when they began to be used as preserving agents for fruits, fish and fowl. Most of the classic liqueurs only came into being around the 1700s, but it was during the classic epoch of French gastronomy in the 1800s when wine, spirits and liqueurs finally found their rightful place in the dishes as well as the glasses of the table.

Today, there is quite a lot of negative publicity about alcohol in matters of health, and a lot of it is misinformed rubbish, particularly about wine. Much of the misinformation being fed into the system blatantly ignores

8

the serious scientific research that has shown beyond doubt that a moderate wine drinker will have a healthier life than a teetotaller.

A little alcohol in your food and a little in your glass to go with it will do no harm at all, and you will have a far more enjoyable life than those who would have you forswear it.

CHAPTER 1

Red Wine

The Very Best Coq au Vin

One of the most amusing meals I have eaten was in the Armagnac brandy region of south-western France. We had been tasting Armagnacs all one chilly winter's morning, and were fired up and ready to eat. Our hosts took us to what appeared from the outside to be a railway station. It was, but a de-commissioned one. We had to buy a one franc ticket to get in, all the staff were done up as railway buffet staff, and about every 20 minutes, they ran a tape of a train approaching and stopping at the station.

Gastronomically, you would have grave doubts about such a venue, but a glance around revealed it was chock full of locals, an encouraging sign. In fact, the food turned out to be very good, with a marvellous coq au vin as the main course. It inspired me to start cooking the dish myself.

This is a fantastic coq au vin with a really dark sauce. You need to marinate the chicken pieces overnight in wine, before cooking it the next day. It is even better served the day after that. Use a good chicken for the best taste.

SERVES 4

3¹/₂lb/1.6kg oven-ready
  chicken, in 8 pieces
3oz/75g butter
1 tbsp oil
4 thick slices streaky bacon,
  rinded and diced
8 shallots, peeled and left
  whole
4 tbsp Armagnac

2 cloves garlic, peeled and
  crushed
bouquet garni
¹/₄pt/150ml chicken stock
1 tbsp plain flour
4oz/100g small button
  mushrooms, wiped
1 tbsp finely chopped fresh
  parsley

13

For the marinade

1³/4pt (1 litre) red wine
  (preferably something
  full-bodied and deeply
  coloured)
1 onion, peeled and sliced

3 cloves garlic, peeled and
  crushed
3 sprigs fresh parsley
8 black peppercorns, bruised
1 bay leaf

Trim away any chicken fat. Place pieces in a bowl and mix with the marinade ingredients. Cover and leave in the fridge for at least 12 hours. Turn the chicken over once or twice.

Next day remove chicken pieces, and strain and reserve the marinade. Melt 2oz/50g butter and the oil in a pan and fry chicken pieces until browned all over. Drain on kitchen paper and place in a flameproof casserole. Add bacon and shallots to the pan and cook over medium heat until both are browning. Remove to casserole with a slotted spoon. Add Armagnac to pan and tilt pan to ignite. When flames have died down, add about a wine glass of wine from the marinade, the garlic and bouquet garni. Stir to scrape up any sediment or juices in the pan while bubbling. Pour over chicken with remaining marinade and stock. Bring to the boil, then turn down to simmer for about 1¹/2 hours with the lid askew.

Meanwhile mix the remaining butter with the flour to make a paste. Add little pieces of this paste to the liquor, stirring. This will slightly thicken the sauce. Add mushrooms, then continue cooking for another 15 minutes, uncovered, until sauce is reduced and dark, and chicken is cooked through. Serve sprinkled with chopped parsley.

Wine: Well, it has to be red, but I would go for something lighter like a decent Beaujolais or a Merlot-dominated wine.

Chicken, Prawn and Monkfish Stew

When it comes to paprika, the Hungarians have no peers. I once spent a week travelling around the Hungarian vineyards, and every dish we were offered either had paprika in it or sprinkled over it. If they could make paprika-flavoured beer, the Hungarians would do it.

At the end of the trip we had a fascinating hour wandering around the Budapest food market, and I was able to buy a satisfyingly large bag of paprika as a souvenir.

This is no Hungarian recipe, but paprika is a key flavouring element. The unusual flavour combinations of the fish and chicken marry well in a robust sauce which is enriched with almonds.

SERVES 4

4 tbsp oil
1 onion, peeled and finely chopped
1 red pepper, seeded and cut into squares
3 cloves garlic, peeled and finely chopped
2 chicken breast fillets, in large chunks
2 tbsp paprika
1lb/450g monkfish fillet, in chunks

5 tomatoes, skinned and chopped
1 wine glass red wine
4oz/100g large prawns, peeled
2 tbsp ground almonds
8 whole basil leaves
salt and freshly ground black pepper
good squeeze lime juice

15

Heat 2 tbsp oil in a pan and gently fry onion, pepper and garlic until softened, but not brown. Remove with a slotted spoon and reserve. Add chicken to pan with remaining oil and fry to seal and brown. Add paprika and stir to mix. Cook 1 minute. Add monkfish and tomatoes. Pour over wine and bring to the boil. Reduce heat. Cover and simmer until fish and chicken are cooked through, about 20 minutes.

Add prawns to stew and bring back to bubbling. Over medium heat, stir in almonds to thicken the sauce. Add basil leaves, and season with salt and freshly ground black pepper. Add a squeeze of lime juice and serve immediately.

WINE: Despite the fish influence, this is more a red wine dish. Try a red from northern Spain, such as a Penedès.

Rosy Chicken

I went once on a press trip to see one of the leading rosé producers in the south of France. They decided to give us a treat and cooked a cargolade. *For the uninitiated, and I certainly was, this is a snail barbecue with the snails grilled over a fire of dried vine prunings.*

Apart from our hosts being seriously into garlic, this was fine, and the snails, served with freshly baked bread, were delicious. However, our appreciation of the snails was rather ruined when one of our party who, despite being a serious eater, had not touched his snails, burst into tears at the table. Heaving with sobs he explained he had a pet snail called Tim. I kid you not.

No snails in this, but the sauce is made from rosé. A delicious dinner party dish of chicken breast fillets simply cooked in rosé with green peppercorns, and served on rösti with snow peas.

SERVES 4

1 tbsp oil
2oz/50g butter
1 onion, peeled and finely chopped
4 skinned chicken breast fillets

3 wine glasses dry rosé
4 tsp green peppercorns
salt and freshly ground black pepper
8oz/225g snow peas, trimmed

FOR THE RÖSTI
2 large potatoes
1 onion, peeled and grated

oil for frying

Heat oil and butter in a pan and fry onion over gentle heat until softened, but not brown. Add chicken and cook on both sides until golden and sealed. Pour over rosé and add green peppercorns. Season with salt and freshly ground black pepper. Bring to the boil, then turn down heat, cover with a lid and simmer until chicken is cooked through, about 15 minutes.

Meanwhile make the rösti. Peel and grate the potato on the fine holes of the grater or processor. Place in a bowl with grated onion. Season well. Divide the mix into two. Heat oil in a pan and gently drop the potato mix in, spreading out with the back of a spoon to make two flat cakes. Fry gently until brown on each side.

Meanwhile cook snow peas in boiling salted water until just tender.

Take the lid off the chicken pan and bring to bubbling

until sauce is reduced by a third.

Remove chicken breasts and slice thickly. Arrange on rösti on two warmed plates with snow peas tucked in between the slices. Pour over sauce.

WINE: A dry southern French rosé from Provence or Tavel. These rosés have a 'saltiness' about them which others lack.

Penne Arrabbiata alla Nadia

At the magazine I used to edit, we held frequent wine tastings, and as part of their meagre reward for attending, we used to invite the tasters to lunch at the office.

One day a new recruit to the editorial team volunteered to make lunch and came up with this simple but delicious recipe.

Quill pasta in a tongue-tingling chilli sauce.

SERVES 4

1 large onion, peeled and
  finely chopped
4 cloves garlic, peeled and
  crushed
1 red pepper, seeded and
  diced
2 red chillies, seeded and
  finely chopped
3 tbsp olive oil

14oz/400g can chopped
  tomatoes
4 tbsp tomato purée
4oz/100g Italian salami,
  skinned and crumbled or
  diced
2 wine glasses red wine,
  preferably Italian
2 bay leaves

salt and freshly ground black
pepper
18oz/500g penne pasta

freshly grated Parmesan
cheese

Gently fry onion, garlic, pepper and chillies in olive oil until softened. Add tomatoes and cook for 5 minutes. Stir in tomato purée. Add salami, wine and bay leaves. Bring to the boil, lower heat and simmer for 30 minutes or until the sauce is thickened. Add extra wine if necessary. Season with salt and freshly ground black pepper.

While the sauce is cooking, boil pasta in lightly salted water until al dente. Drain, and transfer to a bowl. Pour over sauce and toss to coat. Serve with freshly grated Parmesan for sprinkling.

WINE: Decent Chianti Classico.

Wendy's Spaghetti Bolognaise

I am sure the good citizens of Bologna have never made this version of their famous ragu, or sauce, because an essential ingredient is cabbage. My mother, from whom the recipe came, tells me they do, but never in my lifetime have I seen it in Italy, or anywhere else. Nevertheless it is a delicious, hearty sauce, and the leftovers taste great on toast the next day.

A slightly unorthodox, but excellent pasta sauce.

SERVES 2

1 Spanish onion, peeled
4 tbsp olive oil
2 cloves garlic, peeled and
    crushed
8oz/225g best-quality lean
    mince
salt and freshly ground black
    pepper
7oz/200g can chopped
    tomatoes
juice and finely grated zest of
    1/2 lemon
2 bay leaves
1 tbsp finely chopped fresh
    parsley

1 tbsp tomato purée
good dash Worcestershire
    sauce
1 heaped tsp Marmite or
    Vegemite
1/2 bottle red wine
4oz/100g white cabbage,
    finely shredded
6oz/175g spaghetti
freshly grated Parmesan
extra chopped parsley and
    lemon juice to serve

Thinly slice the onion after you have helped yourself to a glass of the wine. Heat a little olive oil in a pan and add the onion and garlic. Cook over gentle heat until they become transparent, but not brown. Remove from pan with a slotted spoon and reserve.

Add a little more oil to the pan and then add the mince. Using a spatula or wooden spoon, crumble the mince until there are no lumpy bits, and the mince begins to change colour. Add a few serious twists of freshly ground black pepper. Pour over tomatoes. Squeeze in the lemon juice and add zest and herbs.

Here, I usually throw in a good squirt of tomato purée, a dash of Worcestershire sauce and a heaped teaspoon of Marmite. Now add enough red wine to cover everything in the pan. Add the finely shredded cabbage. Simmer with the lid on for about an hour, stirring occasionally,

20

adding a dash more red wine when the mixture looks too thick.

Next cook the spaghetti in plenty of boiling salted water until just tender. Drain and add a little more olive oil. Meanwhile take the lid off the pan and reduce the sauce slightly. Check seasoning.

Serve sauce on pasta. Sprinkle with freshly grated Parmesan cheese, a little freshly chopped parsley and another squeeze of lemon juice.

WINE: A good young Chianti would be perfect, though almost any red wine with a bit of body will go well with this dish.

Whole Stuffed Cabbage

I am not sure what the origins of this hearty winter warmer are, but I first ate it in Italy. As it was cooked by an Australian friend of mine, the issue was confused. It was a freezing cold day, and we had been playing bocce, the Italian equivalent of boules. To keep the inner fires going, we had been drinking grappa, the brandy made from wine-making leftovers (skins, stalks, etc). Grappa sneaks up on you, and it sure did this day. When Anthea saw the condition of the players coming off the bocce court, she decided they needed some ballast before things got out of hand, and produced the following dish.

SERVES 4

2 tbsp oil	1 wine glass red wine
1 onion, peeled and finely	¼pt/150ml beef stock
chopped	few fresh thyme leaves,
2 cloves garlic, peeled and	chopped
crushed	2oz/50g cooked white rice
12oz/350g best minced beef	salt and freshly ground black
7oz/200g can chopped	pepper
tomatoes	1 whole green cabbage
2 tbsp tomato purée	melted butter for brushing

Heat oil in a large pan. Gently fry onion and garlic until softened. Remove with a slotted spoon and reserve. Add mince to pan and fry to brown.

Return onion and garlic to pan and stir in chopped tomatoes, tomato purée, wine, stock and thyme. Bring to the boil. Lower heat and simmer gently for 20 minutes. Stir in rice and season with salt and freshly ground black pepper.

Meanwhile, trim the stalk of the cabbage, but leave it whole. Cook in lightly salted boiling water until just tender, about 15 minutes. Drain and cool slightly. Carefully unfurl the leaves, folding them back, and removing some in the centre to make a cavity. Reserve these for another recipe or chop and add them to the mince. Stuff the centre with mince mixture. Brush cabbage with melted butter and place in the preheated oven at Gas 6/400°F/200°C for 15 minutes or until thoroughly hot.

WINE: A light, crisp, dry white, such as a Vinho Verde.

Red Meat Marinade

Almost every Australian home has a barbecue. Mine is a Weber, a fire-engine-red little number that is very versatile. Not only can you grill on it, you can also do spit roasts. The day before it gets fired up, I like to marinate the meats I am going to cook using this recipe. It is suitable for all red meats, and helps keep the meat moist.

FOR 4 STEAKS

3/4pt/450ml red wine
2 cloves garlic, bruised
1 onion, peeled and sliced
1 fresh bouquet garni
   (including 1 bay leaf, few
   sprigs parsley and thyme)

2 tbsp oil
few bruised black
   peppercorns

Place steaks in a shallow dish. Mix marinade ingredients and pour over. Leave, covered, in the fridge for 1 hour. Baste with marinade during cooking.

WINE: Chunky red wines like those from southern France and southern Italy, or Australian Shiraz, accompany marinated steaks well.

Whittington's Old-Fashioned Beef and Scallop Pie

One of the teeth-grinding gastronomic developments of recent years has been the advent of establishments that bill themselves as 'surf and turf' restaurants, though horse never features on the menu. Who would want to eat in such a place?

Nevertheless, this recipe should satisfy those devotees of the genre and many others as well.

The quaint mix of tastes in this pie is surprisingly good, especially topped with this crisp pastry.

SERVES 6

4 tbsp oil
1 onion, peeled and finely chopped
3 cloves garlic, peeled and crushed
2lb/900g lean chuck steak, in cubes
seasoned flour
1 sprig fresh thyme, chopped

1 tbsp finely chopped fresh parsley
1 bay leaf
$1/2$pt/300ml beef stock
2 wine glasses red wine
salt and freshly ground black pepper
8 fresh shelled scallops, sliced
beaten egg to glaze

FOR THE PASTRY
6oz/175g plain flour
pinch salt

4oz/100g unsalted butter, chilled and in cubes
1 egg, beaten

24

Heat 2 tbsp oil in a pan and gently fry onion and garlic over low heat until soft. Transfer to a flameproof casserole. Dip beef in seasoned flour and shake off excess. Add remaining oil to frying pan and add beef in batches to seal and brown over high heat. Transfer to casserole. Add herbs and pour over stock and wine. Season with salt and freshly ground black pepper. Bring to just bubbling, not boiling, then lower heat and simmer covered for around 1¹/2 hours or until beef is tender. Remove lid and continue bubbling gently over low heat for about 15 minutes for the sauce to reduce a little and thicken slightly.

While the beef is cooking make the pastry. Place all ingredients except egg in a processor and whizz until the pastry forms a ball. Remove from processor, wrap in film, and chill for 30 minutes.

Add scallops to casserole at the end of cooking time and remove from heat and cool. Transfer to a pie dish.

Roll out pastry on a lightly floured board to fit the top of the pie dish. From the trimmings, cut a strip to attach to the rim of the pie dish with water. Attach pastry lid to the rim with more water. Pinch edges to seal. Roll out remaining trimmings to make decorations for the top. Attach these to the top and glaze all over with beaten egg. Bake in the preheated oven at Gas 5/375°F/190°C for 35 minutes, or until the crust is crisp, shiny and golden, and filling is hot.

WINE: A hearty dish like this needs a hearty red wine. Try any Californian or Australian red that is not Merlot-driven. A Cape Pinotage would also go well.

Beef Casserole with Prunes

Growing up in Australia, beef was an integral part of the daily diet. Some would say I should count my blessings, and quite right they would be too. However, as a youngster, beef meant two things, roast or steak. Roast lamb or lamb chops, or the odd chicken that my father decided to knock on the head, were the only real alternatives.

In the 1950s, Australia was seriously British. The then Prime Minister, Robert Menzies, would never have dared pat the Queen on the bum. Yet despite our Britishness, such dishes as Lancashire hotpot and others that used meats in a creative way never seemed to see the light of day. Or not in my experience. This dish, with an unlikely combination of beef and prunes, is rather good.

Slow-simmered beef cooked with red wine, bacon and prunes which add a certain sweet fruitiness to the gravy.

SERVES 4

2 tbsp oil
1oz/25g butter
4 rashers back bacon, rinded and chopped
2lb/900g chuck steak, in cubes
2 onions, peeled and finely chopped
2 carrots, peeled and sliced
¹/₂pt/300ml red wine

¹/₄pt/150ml beef stock
1 tbsp finely chopped fresh parsley
4oz/100g pitted no-soak prunes
salt and freshly ground black pepper
freshly grated Parmesan cheese for sprinkling

Heat oil and butter in a deep pan and fry bacon crisp. Remove and reserve. Add steak cubes in batches, frying to brown and seal. Remove and reserve these too. Lower heat and fry onions and carrots gently for about 5 minutes. Return meat and bacon to pan and pour over wine and stock. Bring to just bubbling and then lower heat. Add parsley. Cover and simmer for 2¹/₂ hours or until beef is tender. Add prunes halfway through cooking time. Keep an eye on it and add more wine and stock if necessary. Season with salt and freshly ground black pepper. Serve sprinkled with freshly grated Parmesan cheese.

WINE: Because the prunes add a sweetness, a light and fruity red wine like a good Beaujolais (not *nouveau*), or the Piedmontese Dolcetto d'Alba would go very well.

Boeuf à la Bourgignonne

The Burgundians can be an odd lot. I once went to a special lunch at a famous London restaurant at the invitation of a leading producer of Burgundy. The object was to convince a group of wine writers that the wines from a recent vintage were not as bad as we were making them out to be, and would we stop whingeing about the prices. What made the lunch stay in my mind, apart from the fact that we were right about the wines, was that every course except dessert involved veal. Perhaps the producer thought that this was going to help his wines along, but it didn't.

The Burgundians may have lost the plot when it comes to their wines, but this recipe remains a classic.

Brilliant stew of chunks of tender beef marinated and cooked in red Burgundy.

SERVES 4

2lb/900g chuck steak,
  trimmed and cubed
1 bottle red Burgundy or
  other red wine
5 tbsp oil
4 rashers streaky bacon,
  rinded and chopped
2 tbsp seasoned flour
1 onion, peeled and finely
  chopped
2 cloves garlic, peeled and
  crushed

12 baby onions, peeled
1/4pt/150ml beef stock
1 tbsp finely chopped fresh
  parsley
few thyme sprigs, chopped
1 bay leaf
4oz/100g button
  mushrooms, wiped
salt and freshly ground black
  pepper
extra chopped parsley for
  decoration

For the marinade
red wine, see above
1 tbsp oil
1 onion, peeled and chopped

2 bay leaves
few black peppercorns
2 cloves garlic, bruised

Place beef in a bowl and mix with the marinade ingredients using half of the wine. Leave to marinate for 4 hours or preferably overnight, turning the meat once or twice. Strain beef and reserve liquid, discarding flavourings. Pat beef dry.

Heat 3 tbsp oil in a pan and fry bacon crisp. Remove with a slotted spoon and transfer to a flameproof casserole. Reserve. Dip beef in seasoned flour and shake off excess. Add to frying pan in batches to seal and brown. Place in casserole. Lower heat and add remaining oil to frying pan. Cook chopped onion and garlic gently until softened. Add to beef. Fry baby onions to brown and place in casserole. Pour over remaining wine from the bottle and the reserved marinade and stock. Bring to the boil, then lower heat. Add parsley, thyme and bay leaf, then simmer gently for 2½ hours or until beef is tender.

About 20 minutes before end of cooking time add mushrooms. Season with salt and freshly ground black pepper. Sprinkle over extra chopped parsley to decorate just before serving.

Wine: It would be churlish not to suggest red Burgundy and put a few francs in the pockets of the hapless producers, but if you are feeling less than friendly towards the Burgundians, serve a decent Pinot Noir from anywhere.

Hungarian Goulasch

In Australia, we have a rather civilised thing called the wine box or cask, which is filtering out to the rest of the world. Basically it is a cardboard box with an aluminium bladder holding the wine and a tap that is designed to keep air out. The standard size is 4 litres (about 7 pints), and they are cheap. You can have a glass when you like, and have red and white wine to hand when you are cooking without having to open a bottle.

When the boxes first came out, the producers had to reassure a sceptical public that the wine would not go off. So they put a claimer on the box that the wine would last for at least three months. One irate punter phoned to say that in his household the bloody casks only seemed to last about three days!

Robust stew flavoured with paprika and caraway.

SERVES 4

5 tbsp oil
1 large onion, peeled and
 chopped
3 cloves garlic, peeled and
 crushed
1½lb/700g chuck steak,
 trimmed and cubed
seasoned flour
1 large carrot, peeled and
 sliced

14oz/400g can chopped
 tomatoes
1½ wine glasses red wine
1 tbsp tomato purée
2 level tbsp paprika
1 tsp caraway seeds
salt and freshly ground black
 pepper
1 tbsp white wine vinegar
2 tbsp soured cream

Heat 2 tbsp oil in a flameproof casserole and fry onion and garlic over gentle heat until softened. Remove with a slotted spoon and reserve. Dip steak in seasoned flour and shake off excess. Add remaining oil to casserole and fry steak in batches to brown. Do not crowd the pan. Return all meat, onion and garlic to the casserole. Add carrot, and pour over tomatoes and wine. Next add tomato purée, paprika, caraway seeds and seasoning.

Bring to simmering, then turn down to low, covered, for 1¹/₂ hours, or until meat is tender. Add vinegar 10 minutes before the end of cooking time. Drizzle over soured cream before serving.

WINE: An Australian Shiraz, or something chunky from the south of France.

Roast Beef and Yorkshire Pudding with Perfect Gravy

Every cook should have a roast in his or her repertoire for that family occasion. My favourite happens to be beef, because the cold meat is tasty, too. Beef also gives me the excuse to visit the cellar and rummage around for a decent, mature bottle of wine.

When buying your beef, make sure you get the butcher to weigh it for you as the cooking time will depend on the weight. If you are wondering where the wine is in this dish, it's in the gravy, which is the next recipe!

Traditional roast served with fail-safe airy Yorkshire puddings and a rich gravy.

SERVES 6

5lb/2.2kg beef rib roast
salt and freshly ground black
 pepper

oil
The Perfect Gravy (see next
 recipe)

FOR THE PUDDING
4oz/100g plain flour   *2 eggs, beaten*
pinch salt   *1/2pt/300ml milk*

First make the Yorkshire pudding batter. Sift flour and
salt into a bowl and make a well in the middle. Whisk in
eggs with a little of the milk until you have a smooth
batter. Gradually stir in remaining milk. Chill in the
fridge for 15 minutes.

Next, preheat oven to the highest possible temperature. Rub a little salt into the beef fat on the outside and
grind over lots of freshly milled pepper. Place beef in a
roasting tray and brush with a little oil. Roast for 15
minutes at the high heat, basting. Remove beef from
oven and reduce heat to Gas 5/375°F/190°C. Return beef
to oven and start timing from this point. If you like your
beef rare, allow 15 minutes per 1lb/450g, 20 minutes for
medium, and 25 for well-done. Remove from oven to
'rest' and keep warm. This makes it easy to carve and
keeps the juices in.

To make the Yorkshires, turn up oven to Gas 7/425°F/
220°C. Heat some oil in a patty pan until very hot. Pour
batter into holes and return to oven. Cook for 15
minutes, or until puddings are billowing, crisp and
golden. Serve around the meat.

WINE: A decent mature claret is perfect, but a good
Cabernet Sauvignon, old Chianti Classico, Barolo or
Rioja would go well.

The Perfect Gravy

Over the years I have built up a cellar of mature wines and vintage ports, both of which need decanting. I never throw away the sediment, but keep it in an empty Spanish brandy bottle. It makes a great addition to the gravy.

Which reminds me of a story. The elderly widow of a distinguished gentleman contacted his former wine merchants. She wanted to know if they had any more Cockburns 1927 port. The young salesman said, No, they did not, but they had the 1945 Cockburns, which was just as good. She ordered ten cases at quite considerable cost. Several days later she phoned the salesman asking him to take the wine back as it was no good. As the 1945 vintage was the greatest this century, the salesman was rather stunned. When he asked what was wrong with it, she replied that it did not have lots of that stuff at the bottom of the bottle. She explained that she did not like the port, but loved spreading the sediment on toast. The salesman almost fainted at the thought of her pouring away some of the greatest wine of the century – just to get at the sediment.

You need the pan juices, beef stock – and wine, with sediment if possible.

½oz/15g plain flour
½tsp English mustard
powder, or to taste
1 wine glass red wine with a
little sediment, if possible

½pt/300ml beef stock
salt and freshly ground black
pepper

Remove beef from roasting pan. Pour off excess fat into a small bowl and reserve for dripping. Leave to set.

Sprinkle flour into meat juices in the roasting pan. Stir to incorporate and place over gentle heat for a minute, stirring. Add mustard. Pour over wine (and a little sediment) and stock and bring to the boil, stirring. Bubble until slightly thickened and reduced. Strain, then season with salt and freshly ground black pepper. Pour into a warmed gravy boat and serve.

Braised Oxtail 'Gwynn Jones'

My wedding reception was held at a wonderful London restaurant called Pomegranates, and a decade later so was my 'divorce' party. Over the intervening years I became firm friends with the owner, Patrick Gwynn Jones, who has created one of the most eclectic menus ever, with dishes from all over the world. It is a menu that has so many dishes you want to try that it takes ages to choose. Patrick is quite happy about this, as he usually manages to sell you a bottle of Champagne to drink while you mull over the menu.

Over the decade or more I have dined at Pomegranates, I have managed to try many of Patrick's creations – his börek pastries with fiery chilli sauce, his goat curry, his Welsh lamb with onions. His braised oxtail became one of my winter favourites, and this is his recipe.

Oxtail needs long and slow cooking, but the end result is a reputation-making dish of amazing meaty richness and intense flavour. This can be prepared the day before, which is probably best because the rich flavour is even more intense the next day.

SERVES 4

2¹/₂lb/1.1kg oxtail pieces
seasoned flour
5 tbsp oil
2 onions, peeled and finely sliced
2 cloves garlic, peeled and crushed
2 leeks, trimmed and sliced

3 carrots, peeled and sliced
2 sticks celery, chopped
1 bottle inexpensive red wine
2 bay leaves
few sprigs fresh thyme, chopped
6 cloves
12 black peppercorns

36

1/4pt/150ml beef stock
7oz/200g can chopped
  tomatoes
salt and freshly ground black
  pepper

finely chopped fresh parsley
  for decoration

Dip oxtail in seasoned flour and shake off excess. Heat 3 tbsp oil in a pan and fry oxtail pieces all over to brown and seal. Remove and place in an ovenproof casserole. Add remaining oil to pan and gently fry onions and garlic over low heat to soften. Lift out with a slotted spoon and place these in casserole. Add leek, carrot and celery to frying pan and cook until they begin to caramelise. Transfer to casserole. Pour red wine into frying pan and stir to scrape up any meat juices. Bring to the boil, pour over oxtail and vegetables. Add bay leaves, thyme, cloves, peppercorns and pour over beef stock.

Cover casserole with a tight-fitting lid and place in the preheated oven at Gas 3/325°F/160°C for at least 4 hours, or until oxtail is tender. The secret of this recipe is the long slow cooking which tenderises the meat and releases the juices to make a rich gravy. Half an hour before end of cooking time, add tomatoes and season with salt and freshly ground black pepper. When the meat is tender, it can be removed from the oven and cooled, then placed in the fridge overnight.

Reheat gently over low to medium heat, bringing to bubbling point to heat thoroughly before serving. Serve in bowls decorated with chopped parsley. Creamy mashed potato is the best accompaniment.

WINE: A rich red like an Italian Barolo, Australian Shiraz or Californian Zinfandel.

Moussaka

My mother once phoned me in London to ask if I knew of a good hotel in Athens. I did – a nice little place on the edge of the Plaka, with sweeping views up to the Parthenon, and big balconies on the top floor where you could have a sundowner and take in the view. She asked me to book her and a girlfriend in, which I did. Some time later, when she reached London, she told me what a lovely hotel it was and how nice the owner was. But she said she was puzzled about why at night the lobby was filled with old men. It was then I told her she had been staying in a brothel, tourists only on the top floor.

I always think of that hotel when I make moussaka.

Best made with lean minced lamb, but you can substitute beef. This version with red wine is particularly good.

SERVES 4

2 medium aubergines, sliced
   into thin circles
salt and freshly ground black
   pepper
5 tbsp oil
1 large onion, peeled and
   finely chopped

1lb/450g lean lamb mince
3 cloves garlic, peeled and
   crushed
14oz/400g can tomatoes
1 wine glass red wine
1 tsp fresh rosemary,
   chopped

FOR THE SAUCE
2oz/50g butter
2oz/50g plain flour
1/2pt/300ml milk

1 egg
2oz/50g Cheddar cheese,
   grated

Place aubergines in a colander and sprinkle with salt. Leave for 30 minutes, rinse, drain and pat dry on kitchen paper.

Meanwhile, make the sauce. Melt butter in a pan and add flour. Cook over medium heat for 1 minute – don't let it brown. Gradually add the milk, stirring all the time, and simmer over low heat, still stirring, until thick. Season. Take off the heat, and place a circle of greaseproof paper on top to stop a skin forming.

Next, heat 3 tbsp oil and quickly fry aubergine slices until golden on both sides. Drain on kitchen paper. Reserve. Add remaining oil to the pan and gently fry onion until soft but not brown. Add mince and garlic and fry until meat is browned. Add tomatoes, red wine and rosemary. Season with salt and freshly ground black pepper. Continue cooking until most of the liquid has gone.

Place a layer of aubergine slices in a shallow baking dish. Cover with the mince, then place remaining aubergine slices on top.

Remove greaseproof paper from sauce. Gradually beat egg into the sauce. Pour this over the aubergine slices. Sprinkle over cheese. Bake in the preheated oven at Gas 4/350°F/180°C for 45 minutes.

WINE: Retsina if you like the stuff, which I do not, or go for a decent Greek red wine to keep the mood. A New Zealand or South African Cabernet will go just as well.

Pan-Fried Lamb and Celery

This is a good dinner party dish, with a vaguely Mediterranean feel to it, and is reasonably easy on the calories. I often wonder why so much fuss is made about calories in these modern times. When I was growing up, parents thought it was more important to make sure the children were fed well so they would grow up strong and healthy. They had never heard of anorexia, or the other diseases associated with weight, and there was a lot of tut-tutting over skinny children on the grounds their parents were not feeding them well enough. Perhaps they had the right attitude.

Noisettes of lamb with thinly sliced celery in a vibrant red pepper sauce. This is a quick, easy, and delicious way to serve lamb.

SERVES 4

1 head celery
3 tbsp oil

12 lamb noisettes

FOR THE SAUCE
1 tbsp oil
2 red peppers, seeded and in chunks
1 clove garlic, peeled and crushed

1/4pt/150ml vegetable stock
1 wine glass red wine
salt and freshly ground black pepper

First make the sauce. Heat oil in a pan and gently fry peppers and garlic until softened. Add stock and wine, then continue cooking until completely tender and the liquid is reduced by half. Whizz smooth and season with salt and freshly ground black pepper. Reserve.

Next cook the celery. Trim the head, then slice into 3in (7.5cm) lengths. Heat oil in a pan and fry slices on both sides until brown. Blot on kitchen paper and keep warm. Finally fry noisettes on both sides until brown outside and pink in the centre, or to preference, then season.

Heat sauce through and pour in a puddle on four plates. Place noisettes on top and tumble celery over.

WINE: Red Rioja or, in tribute to one of the great sheep-producing countries of the world, a New Zealand Cabernet Sauvignon.

Lamb Cutlets with Garlic and Parsley

As Australia has more sheep per head than any country other than New Zealand, lamb was a regular visitor to our family table, either as chops or as a roast. The chops were always helped along by a liberal libation from the tomato sauce bottle. I wish my mother had known about this sauce instead.

A flavourful way to deal with lamb cutlets. Cook them with garlic and serve with a rich wine and parsley gravy.

SERVES 4

3 cloves garlic, peeled
12 lamb cutlets, trimmed
salt and freshly ground black
  pepper
2 tbsp oil
1 wine glass red wine

2 tbsp finely chopped fresh
  parsley
1/4pt/150ml lamb stock
extra chopped fresh parsley
  for decoration

Crush 2 cloves garlic and spread a little over the cutlets –
you literally just need a smear. Season them with freshly
ground black pepper. Heat oil in a pan and cook cutlets to
preference. Remove from the pan and keep warm.

Pour excess oil from pan, keeping the meat juices.
Pour wine into the pan, stirring to scrape up any sediment. Bring to bubbling, then add parsley, remaining
crushed garlic and stock. Simmer until reduced by a
third. Season. Place cutlets on warmed plates and pour
gravy around. Sprinkle extra parsley over for decoration.

WINE: A young claret or any lighter Cabernet Sauvignon
is a good choice. The New Zealand or Bulgarian versions
tend towards the lighter style.

Superlative Shepherd's Pie

The late Michael Smith was a quintessential Englishman and he believed English cuisine had been unjustly maligned. He did much research into the history of English cuisine and the dishes of days past. He used those researches to write articles and books about the lineage of English gastronomy and, virtually alone, put those traditions back on the map.

Michael also recreated some historic dishes for two landmark London restaurants, Walton's and The English House. Shepherd's pie was one of his favourites, and he described it as being to Britain what lasagne is to Italy.

A midweek supper dish or a dinner party special, shepherd's pie is always a great choice, especially topped with luxury mash.

SERVES 4

2 tbsp oil
1 large onion, peeled and
   finely chopped
1¹/₂lb/700g best lamb or beef
   mince
3 tbsp tomato purée
dash Worcestershire sauce

1 tbsp finely chopped fresh
   parsley
¹/₄pt/150ml red wine
¹/₂pt/300ml lamb or beef
   stock
salt and freshly ground black
   pepper

FOR THE MASH TOPPING
2lb/900g potatoes, peeled
   and in chunks
1¹/₂oz/40g butter
3 tbsp double cream

freshly grated nutmeg
2oz/50g mature Cheddar
   cheese, grated

Heat oil in a pan and gently cook onion until golden. Remove with a slotted spoon and drain on kitchen paper. Add mince to the pan and fry brown. Return onion to pan and stir. Add tomato purée, Worcestershire sauce and parsley. Pour over wine and stock, and season with salt and freshly ground black pepper. Bring to the boil, then turn down heat and bubble until mince mixture becomes thick as liquid has reduced.

Cook potatoes in boiling salted water. Drain and mash well. Beat in butter, cream and a good grating of nutmeg. Season well with salt and pepper.

Spoon mince into an ovenproof dish, then top with mashed potato. Smooth over with the prongs of a fork to make a pattern. Cook in the preheated oven at Gas 6/400°F/200°C for 20 minutes. About 10 minutes before the end of cooking time, sprinkle cheese over the top. Return to oven for this to melt.

WINE: Basically a red wine of your choice. I like to serve one of the more robust wines from the south of France like Languedoc, Corbières, or Minervois.

Daube of Lamb with Chorizo

For several years, I lived with a lady whose parents owned a farm in Australia. They were big on sheep, and one of the annual jobs was to geld the male lambs. This, she told me, involved the use of a knife and her teeth. The name for it, I believe, is 'mulesing'. Anyway, she was very pretty, with a lovely smile, and the odd rogue male used to get interested. I just took them aside and told them about mulesing. It never surprised me that they found something else to do.

A daube is a slow-cooked casserole which takes its name from the special pot, a *daubière*, used to cook it. Originally, it would have been sealed with a flour and water crust, but today, any ovenproof casserole pot with a tight-fitting lid will substitute. This recipe mixes countries – neck of lamb with spicy chorizo sausage, garlic, tomatoes and olives for an intense, rich, flavour – but who cares?

SERVES 4

3 tbsp oil
1 onion, peeled and finely chopped
3 cloves garlic, peeled and crushed
2lb/900g neck of lamb, trimmed
2 wine glasses red wine

14oz/400g can chopped tomatoes
1/4pt/150ml lamb stock
8 thick slices chorizo sausage
1 tbsp fresh rosemary leaves, chopped
12 black olives
salt and freshly ground black pepper

45

Heat oil in a pan and fry onion and garlic until soft but not browned. Remove with a slotted spoon and transfer to an ovenproof casserole. Fry neck of lamb in batches to brown and seal. Transfer to casserole, pour over red wine, tomatoes and stock, and bring to just bubbling. Add chorizo and rosemary and season. Cover and place in the preheated oven at Gas 3/325°F/160°C for 2¹/₂ hours or until lamb is tender.

Stir in olives and season with salt and freshly ground black pepper. Serve with plain boiled potatoes with butter.

WINE: This dish has a Mediterranean flavour, so I would select a decent red Rioja.

Pears in Red Wine

In Alsace, they make a fantastic assortment of clear fruit brandies from all manner of wild and cultivated berries and fruits. The best known is Poire William.

On a visit once, one of our party noticed a bottle of this pear-flavoured brandy in a shop window with a whole pear inside said bottle. She spent the whole of the rest of the trip trying to find out how they got a whole pear through such a narrow aperture. The answer is, of course, that when the pear tree flowers, they place twigs with a flower on, into empty bottles and tie them on to the branches. The fruit develops in the bottles.

This is a simple but classic dessert based on un-bottled pears poached in spiced red wine. Good warm or chilled.

46

SERVES 4

4 even-sized firm ripe pears,
  peeled, with stalks still
  attached
juice of 1 lemon
³/₄pt/450ml red wine

3oz/75g sugar
1 stick cinnamon
pinch mixed spice
3 tsp arrowroot

Slice a layer from the base of each pear, so the pears stand upright. Squeeze a little lemon juice over each one. Pour wine into a deep pan. Add sugar, cinnamon and mixed spice. Slowly bring to bubbling, stirring, until the sugar dissolves.

Lower heat, add pears and cover. Gently poach until fruit is tender, about 12 minutes. Lift pears out with a slotted spoon and transfer to a serving dish. Bring wine back to bubbling. Mix arrowroot to a smooth paste with a little water and stir in. Bring back to the boil, stirring until thickened. Pour some over pears and serve remainder in a sauce boat. Serve warm, or chilled.

WINE: A glass of chilled Poire William, or a sweet white wine like Sauternes.

CHAPTER 2

White Wine

Wild Mushroom Soup

I have come across the odd person who is besotted with mushrooms and will tramp through woods, fields and glens searching for them, as if a treasure hunt were taking place.

The trouble is, you need a good book to distinguish the edible fungi from the ones that are going to do you a serious injury.

I have visions of the late author of such a book having one too many whiskies and getting things mixed up. At least, if you buy your fungi from a shop and get some crook ones, you know whom to sue.

Intensely flavoured soup with foresty flavours. Choose a mix of wild, button and field mushrooms for this. The spicy character of Gewürztraminer is a perfect wine to use in this dish.

SERVES 4

2 tbsp oil

1 onion, peeled and finely chopped

2 cloves garlic, peeled and crushed

1lb/450g mixed mushrooms (wild, button and field), wiped and roughly sliced

1 tbsp finely chopped fresh parsley

1³/₄pt/1 litre chicken stock

2 wine glasses Gewürztraminer

salt and freshly ground black pepper

2 tbsp softly whipped double cream

extra chopped fresh parsley for decoration

Heat oil in a large heavy-bottomed pan and gently fry onion and garlic over low heat until softened but not brown. Add mushrooms and stir for about 2 minutes. Add parsley.

Pour over stock and 1 glass wine. Bring to the boil. Simmer until mushrooms are soft, about 5 minutes. Whizz in a processor or blender. This mix will not purée completely smooth, so blend it to preference.

Return to a clean pan and stir in remaining glass of wine. Reheat gently and season with salt and freshly ground black pepper. Pour into warmed bowls and serve decorated with half a spoonful of soft whipped cream and freshly chopped parsley.

WINE: A decent Pinot Noir, Australian Chardonnay, or amontillado sherry.

Celery and Leek Soup

If you ever want to know why the French are, by and large, better cooks than the British, it is because they weave a bit of romance into their food. Take the respective names for the leek. In French leeks are called 'poireaux', in English, well, 'leeks'. I mean, trying to impress someone, is it not better to say, 'I have just made a tarte aux poireaux *for lunch', rather than 'How about a leek pie?' I rest my case.*

An easy soup with a Continental flavour in spite of its English name.

SERVES 4

3 tbsp oil
1 onion, peeled and chopped
2 cloves garlic, peeled and
  crushed
1 small head celery, scrubbed
  and chopped
2 leeks, trimmed, chopped
  and washed
1 small potato, peeled and
  chopped

1³/₄pt/1 litre vegetable stock
1 wine glass
  Gewürztraminer
1 tsp finely chopped fresh
  thyme
salt and freshly ground black
  pepper
freshly snipped chives for
  decoration

Heat oil in a pan and fry onion and garlic over gentle heat until softened. Add celery, leeks and potato, then pour over vegetable stock and wine. Add thyme, bring to the boil, then turn down to simmer until vegetables are tender, about 15 minutes. Whizz in a processor until smooth. Season to taste with salt and freshly ground black pepper. Serve decorated with freshly snipped chives.

WINE: An Alsace Gewürztraminer has a great affinity with this soup.

Mussels in White Wine

When I was an adolescent, I used to regard mussels as black things which hung off the pylons of the jetties in the Swan River. Then a new-found friend, whose parents happened to hail from Belgium, showed me they were a food source – one that we locals were overlooking. Later, in London, an elegant lady journalist introduced me to the pleasures of a huge steaming bowl of mussels around a winter table. Thanks, Marijke.

The hardest part of this simple dish is cleaning the mussels. The recipe calls for three glasses of dry white wine, but Marijke – a lethal combination of Dutch origins and Australian upbringing – often used quite a lot more.

SERVES 4

4½lb/2kg fresh live mussels
2 tbsp oil
2oz/50g butter
1 large Spanish onion,
  peeled and roughly
  chopped
3 fat cloves garlic, peeled and
  crushed

3 large wine glasses dry
  white wine
1 tbsp finely chopped fresh
  parsley
salt and freshly ground black
  pepper
extra chopped fresh parsley
  for decoration

Scrub mussels in cold running water, removing the 'beards' and any barnacles with a sharp knife. Discard any mussels with broken shells. Tap the shells of any open mussels. If they close, you can use them. If they stay open, they are dead, so throw these out.

In a very large pan with a lid, heat oil and butter, and gently fry onion and garlic over medium heat until transparent. Add cleaned mussels. Pour over white wine and add parsley, a pinch of salt and lots of freshly ground black pepper. Cover pan with a lid, and bring to the boil over high heat for about 4 minutes. Take off lid a couple of times, and stir mussels. Replace lid and continue cooking until all mussels have opened. Using a slotted spoon, transfer them to a large tureen, or serving bowl. Discard any mussels which remain closed. Bring liquor to the boil for another 3 minutes and pour over mussels. Sprinkle with extra parsley before serving with crusty bread.

WINE: I like Australian Riesling with this dish, but Frascati or Soave would do just as well.

Char-Roasted Vegetables

Most barbecues revolve around meat of some description, or at least they do in Australia, and the veggies are usually confined to foil-wrapped potatoes and tossed salads. This tasty combination provides a good counterfoil, as it were, and sorts out the odd rogue vegetarian friend who may arrive.

While these peppers, tomatoes, aubergines, courgettes, parsnips and quartered onions are slowly roasting, the aroma is quite mouth-watering. They are ready when just charred on both sides. Use any selection of vegetables – preferably of a chunky nature, i.e. not French beans.

SERVES 4

1 red and 1 green pepper
1 aubergine, trimmed
4 courgettes, washed and
    trimmed

2 medium parsnips, scrubbed
    and trimmed
1 Spanish onion
4 firm tomatoes

FOR THE BASTE
1/4pt/150ml sunflower oil
1 wine glass white (or red)
    wine
2 cloves garlic, peeled and
    crushed

1 sprig fresh rosemary,
    bruised
2 sprigs fresh thyme, bruised
salt and freshly ground black
    pepper

First make the baste. Place oil, wine, garlic, rosemary and thyme in a bowl and stir together with salt and freshly ground black pepper.

Halve and seed peppers, thickly slice aubergines, halve courgettes lengthways, halve parsnips lengthways, peel and quarter onion, leave tomatoes whole. Place in one layer on a flat baking tray. Paint with baste.

Cook on the barbecue for about 3 minutes each side, turning once. Baste other side and cook this. Be careful not to overcook – the vegetables should stay firm.

WINE: Rich Australian Chardonnay.

Mushroom Risotto

I have never taken mushrooms all that seriously, so it came as quite a surprise to my awakening gastronomic mind when, around a table in France, a conversation began about truffles. I could not believe grown men would roll their eyes, start salivating, and almost swoon over what, after all, is just a fungus. And they found them with the help of pigs.

I thought it was just another funny little French habit, until a leading Barolo producer invited me over to Piedmont to look at his wines. In the course of the visit, he invited me to lunch. This turned out to be an orgy of food with an endless succession of dishes featuring the local white truffle, which did not stop until the dessert arrived. They even have a mushroom brotherhood in those parts.

I still have not come to grips with paying hundreds of dollars for what, after all, is only a fungus. I will stick to the free, quite delicious field variety, thank you.

A serious reputation maker, this is the way to a perfect risotto with the heady flavours of mixed mushrooms, including one large meaty flat mushroom (but not truffles). Use risotto rice for the best results. A good risotto should have a slightly creamy texture and the rice should have a little bite.

SERVES 4

3 tbsp oil
1 onion, peeled and finely
   chopped
2 cloves garlic, peeled and
   crushed

1 large or two small field
   mushrooms (about
   8oz/225g), wiped and
   roughly chopped
8oz/225g risotto rice

salt and freshly ground black
pepper
1pt/600ml chicken or
vegetable stock
1/2pt/300ml dry white wine

8oz/225g button
mushrooms (or a
mixture) finely sliced
1 tbsp finely chopped fresh
parsley

Heat oil in a pan and fry onion and garlic over gentle heat until just soft, but not brown. Add field mushrooms and cook, stirring, for about 5 minutes, still over low heat, until mushrooms are slightly softened.

Stir in rice to coat in the mushroomy mix, and season with salt and freshly ground black pepper. Begin to add mixed stock and wine. This must be done gradually and only add more when the last addition has almost been absorbed. Do not over-stir, or the rice grains will break. When there is about 1/4pt/150ml stock mix left, add button mushrooms and parsley. Add remaining stock and continue cooking gently until stock is absorbed. Adjust seasoning.

WINE: Basically a crisp white wine like Chablis, Bourgogne Blanc, the Tuscan Galestro or, for something with a bit more weight, one of the new Italian Chardonnays.

Cheese Fondue

They say the vineyard owners in Switzerland have one leg shorter than the other so they can get around vineyards without a great deal of discomfort.

When I went on my one and only ski-ing holiday, I was the

chalet girl. The thought of hurtling down a slope at breakneck pace frightens the daylights out of me, and I am quite happy to leave that dubious pleasure to others. So I was delighted to be relegated to the task of preparing meals for a group which had many links with the wine trade. On my first foray to the supermarket, I was horrified to see what they were asking for a bottle of Swiss white wine. It was about what you would pay for a fine white Burgundy, so obviously the Swiss grape growers were over-compensating for the difficulty of their terrain. I bought some cheap Italian wine instead and copped a lot of flak from my friends before I could tell them how much the alternative cost.

Fondue is a very social way of eating as guests can pitch in with the preparation. A fondue pot and spirit burner is useful, but it can also be made in a flameproof casserole over a low burner on the cooker.

SERVES 8

1oz/25g butter	*salt and freshly ground white*
1 fat clove garlic, peeled and	*pepper*
halved	*2 tsp cornflour*
1lb/450g Gruyère cheese,	*4 tbsp Kirsch*
grated	*freshly grated nutmeg*
1lb/450g Emmental cheese,	*2 loaves crusty French bread*
grated	*to serve*
1pt/600ml dry white wine	

Rub the inside of the fondue pot with butter, then with the cut clove of garlic. Put cheeses, wine, salt and freshly ground white pepper in the pot or casserole and place over its burner. (If this is being prepared on a cooker, the heat must be the lowest possible.) Stir continuously until the cheese melts. Slake cornflour with the Kirsch to give a thin paste. Pour this into the melted cheese and continue stirring as mixture thickens slightly and becomes smooth. Add freshly grated nutmeg to taste and extra salt and pepper if necessary.

To eat, guests take a long-handled fork (these come with the fondue set in an ideal world, otherwise short-handled forks from the kitchen drawer), and spike cubes of crusty bread on the end. Then twirl it in the cheesy mix, then eat it.

WINE: Needs a white wine with a decent amount of acidity such as New Zealand Sauvignon Blanc, Frascati, Verdicchio, or Soave.

White Wine Fish Marinade

Fish makes a good choice for the barbecue, though I would not suggest you start thinking about a shark. Generally aim for small fish which will serve one person. I like to marinate the cleaned fish for an hour, and before cooking them I place a sprig of dill in the cavity, just a little.

FOR 4 SMALL FISH

3/4pt/450ml dry white wine
juice and zest of 1/2 lemon
1 tbsp oil
1 onion, peeled and sliced

1 clove garlic, peeled and
   crushed
1 tbsp snipped fresh dill
few bruised black
   peppercorns

Place fish in a shallow dish. Combine all ingredients in a
bowl. Pour over fish. Cover and leave in the fridge for an
hour before cooking.

WINE: Serve Muscadet, New Zealand Sauvignon Blanc,
Verdicchio with grilled marinated fish.

Flaky Fish Puff Pies

I once had an unfortunate and embarrassing experience when some fish bones became lodged in my throat, and have been wary of fish with fine bones, like trout, ever since. In Australia we have two wonderful fish which have lovely flaky, bone-free flesh – the dhufish and the schnapper – but I have substituted lemon sole for them in this dish.

A dinner party dish, but very easy to do. Meltingly delicious crisp puff pastry cases are like large, square vol-au-vent cases, filled with flakes of lemon sole fillet, prawns, and spring onions in a cream and dill sauce.

SERVES 4

*13oz/375g packet puff
  pastry*
2 tbsp oil
*8 spring onions, trimmed and
  cut into lengths*
*12oz/350g lemon sole fillet,
  skinned and chopped*
2oz/50g best peeled prawns

*4fl oz/100ml dry white
  wine*
1/4pt/150ml double cream
*salt and freshly ground black
  pepper*
*1 tbsp finely chopped fresh
  dill*
beaten egg to glaze

Roll out pastry on a lightly floured board to a thickness of 1/2in/1cm. Cut out four 3in/7.5cm squares. Mark a border on each square with the point of a sharp knife, about 1/2in/1cm away from edges, without cutting right through. Lay squares on a greased baking sheet and chill for 30 minutes.

    Meanwhile, make the filling. Heat oil in a pan and fry spring onions gently until softened. Lift out with a slotted spoon and reserve. Add lemon sole and toss around until fish is almost cooked through. Return onion to pan and add prawns. Pour over wine and cream, bring to the boil and reduce slightly. Season with salt and freshly ground black pepper, and add dill. Reserve filling, keeping hot.

Brush pastry with beaten egg and bake in the preheated oven at Gas 6/400°F/200°C for 15 minutes or until risen and golden. Lift out the square in the centre of each pastry case made by cutting the border, and remove a few layers of the pastry underneath. This will make a cavity for the filling. Place pastry cases on individual plates and fill with hot sole and prawn mix. Pour a little sauce over filling before serving. Replace pastry lids. Serve any remaining sauce separately in a sauceboat.

WINE: Muscadet, Sancerre or Chablis.

Pot au Feu

I was invited once by a distinguished member of the British wine trade to visit one of his principals with a view to doing an article on them. It turned out to be the monastery of Chartreuse at Voiron where the monks make that venerable liqueur. It was most interesting as the monks do not let women anywhere near them or their monastery, which rather thwarted the efforts of a lady journalist to get a story.

Our host, Tim, had a serious interest in fine food, and it turned out the trip was more about getting him into the latest Michelin three-star restaurant, than us writing about Chartreuse. He would also make sure we went to the best country restaurant in the vicinity.

Simple version of a robust country dish of chicken, ham, and Savoy cabbage, cooked over low heat with onions in stock.

SERVES 4

3 tbsp oil
1 onion, peeled and roughly
  chopped
2 cloves garlic, peeled and
  crushed
3lb/1.4kg chicken, in 8
  pieces
1 thick slice of ham, in small
  cubes

1/2 head Savoy cabbage,
  sliced
1/2pt/300ml home-made
  chicken stock
1 wine glass dry white wine
salt and freshly ground black
  pepper
finely chopped fresh parsley
  for decoration

Heat 2 tbsp oil in a pan and gently fry onion and garlic over low heat until softened. Remove with a slotted spoon and transfer to a flameproof casserole. Add remaining oil to frying pan and fry chicken pieces on both sides to seal. Transfer to casserole with ham. Add cabbage.

Pour over stock and wine and season with salt and freshly ground black pepper. Cover and simmer gently over medium heat for 30 minutes, or until chicken and cabbage are tender. Serve decorated with freshly chopped parsley.

WINE: Chablis or a white Rioja.

Tony's Florentine Chicken

This, boys, is the one to woo the ladies with. They will never believe you did it. It will establish your reputation as a man not to be gastronomically tinkered with. But be careful you do not find yourself making it more often than you want as the good lady insists on pointing out your finer qualities to a succession of her friends. Even my mother was impressed!

This chicken has a wonderful colourful marbled effect and the flesh – cooked with the spinach and cheese mixture between it and the skin – keeps wonderfully moist.

Serves 4

2lb/900g fresh spinach, washed, trimmed and stalks removed
3¹/₂lb/1.6kg fresh chicken
8oz/225g Ricotta cheese

1 wine glass dry white wine
good dash brandy
salt and freshly ground black pepper
1oz/25g butter, melted

For the stuffing
3 tbsp olive oil
1 onion, peeled and finely chopped
2 cloves garlic, peeled and crushed
4 tbsp fresh white breadcrumbs

grated zest of 1 lemon
1 tbsp freshly snipped chives
1 tbsp finely chopped fresh parsley
Salt and freshly ground black pepper

Cook spinach in a little boiling salted water. Drain, then place between two plates and squeeze as much water out as possible.

Next, start what seems to be the difficult bit – though it isn't. Working from the neck of the chicken, with your fingers gradually tease the skin of the bird away from the flesh of the breast and the top of the drumsticks. Patience is the answer here. Don't bother about the back.

Chop spinach and place in a bowl with Ricotta, working these together to make a green and white paste with half the wine, the brandy, salt and plenty of freshly ground black pepper. Reserve.

For the stuffing, heat 2 tbsp oil in another pan and gently fry onion and garlic until softened. Add bread-crumbs and stir to coat. Add lemon zest, chives, parsley, and seasoning. Add remaining wine.

The next bit is to push the reserved spinach mix gently between the loosened skin of the chicken and the flesh. Then stuff the neck skin with the breadcrumb and herb mixture. Secure underneath the chicken with toothpicks.

Preheat oven to Gas 5/375°F/190°C. Place chicken in a roasting tin, breast side down. Baste with melted butter and remaining olive oil, and cook for 15 minutes. Tilt chicken over and cook the other side of the breast for another 15 minutes. Then finish cooking on its back, still basting, for a further 30 minutes – or until juices run clear when the thigh is pierced with a pointed knife. Allow to cool a little before carving.

WINE: Chablis, or Cape or New Zealand Chardonnay.

Poulet de Loire

I once went over to France to interview the owner of a very distinguished Loire vineyard. The interview took place at the owner's château, and we drank some suitably impressive wines.

After lunch the owner suggested we go outside and have a photograph taken with the flags of our two countries, France and England, fluttering in the background, a sort of entente cordiale photograph. The owner was suitably embarrassed when I told him I was Australian.

This delicious chicken dish is slow-cooked with onions, bacon and Muscadet, a dry white wine from the Loire region. The sauce is enriched with double cream at the end of cooking.

SERVES 4

3lb/1.4kg oven-ready chicken, in 8 pieces	2 cloves garlic, peeled and crushed
salt and freshly ground black pepper	4 sticks celery, washed and chopped
3 tbsp oil	4 carrots, peeled and sliced
2 rashers streaky bacon, rinded and chopped	1oz/25g plain flour
	1/2pt/300ml Muscadet
1 onion, peeled and finely chopped	1/4pt/150ml chicken stock
	4 tbsp double cream

Skin chicken and season with salt and freshly ground black pepper. Heat oil in a deep heavy-bottomed pan and fry chicken over high heat until browned all over. Remove from pan and reserve. Add bacon and fry crisp.

Lift out with a slotted spoon and reserve with chicken. Lower heat and add onion, garlic, celery and carrots. Fry until soft but not brown. Stir in flour and cook for 1 minute. Gradually add wine and stock and stir to mix.

Return chicken and bacon to pan and bring to bubbling. Cover and simmer gently for an hour or until chicken is tender. Stir in cream, then season with salt and freshly ground black pepper.

WINE: Muscadet, Sancerre, or Pouilly Fumé.

Creamy Chicken Gratin

When I cook a chicken, I invariably have leftovers – unless I am entertaining. This dish is an easy way of using up the leftover meat – and any unfinished bottles of white wine which may be hanging around.

A cheap easy, creamy dish using up the dregs of a bottle of white wine.

SERVES 4

2 tbsp oil
1 onion, peeled and finely chopped
1 clove garlic, peeled and crushed
4 flat mushrooms, wiped and sliced

1lb/450g cooked chicken, in medium chunks
good squeeze lemon juice
1 tbsp mature Cheddar cheese, grated
1 tbsp finely chopped fresh parsley

FOR THE SAUCE
1¹/₂oz/40g butter
1¹/₂oz/40g plain flour
³/₄pt/450ml milk
1 wine glass white wine
2 tsp English mustard

2oz/50g mature Cheddar, grated
salt and freshly ground white pepper

First make the sauce. Melt butter in a pan and stir in flour. Cook for 1 minute over gentle heat. Gradually add milk and wine, stirring, and bring to the boil. Keep stirring until sauce thickens. Add mustard and cheese and stir to melt cheese. Season with salt and freshly ground white pepper.

Heat oil in another pan and gently fry onion and garlic until soft but not brown. Add mushrooms and cook for 2 more minutes. Add chicken and stir to mix. Pour over cheese sauce and stir gently. Check seasoning and add a squeeze of lemon juice.

Spoon into an ovenproof dish. Sprinkle with the grated Cheddar and bake in the preheated oven at Gas 6/400°F/200°C for 30 minutes or until top is browned and filling is hot. Sprinkle with chopped parsley for decoration.

WINE: Muscadet or New World Sauvignon Blanc.

Poussins en Papillote

Poussins are great little birds which give an individual serving. 'Spatchcocked' means the birds have been split down the back and opened out.

This charming dish is a surefire winner. The spatchcocked birds are filled with a stuffing of chorizo sausage and cabbage, then wrapped in greaseproof and roasted.

70

SERVES 4

5 tbsp oil	zest and juice of 1 lemon
1 medium Spanish onion, peeled and finely chopped	1 wine glass dry white wine
4oz/100g chorizo sausage	salt and freshly ground black pepper
1/2 small cabbage, core removed and finely shredded	4 poussins
	butter

Heat 2 tbsp oil in a pan and cook onion gently until golden, but not brown. Chop chorizo and add to the pan. Cook 3 minutes more. Add cabbage, lemon zest and wine to the pan and continue cooking until most of the liquid evaporates, but the mix is still moist. Season with salt and freshly ground black pepper. Cool completely.

Open out poussins, by cutting down the back either side of each backbone with kitchen shears. Discard backbones. Season both sides of birds. Sprinkle inside with lemon juice. Leave 10 minutes. Divide stuffing between poussins and fold back up into neat birds. Secure with toothpicks or string.

Lay four sheets of greaseproof paper on a work top and butter them. Place a stuffed poussin on each and brush with remaining oil. Fold over opposite edges of paper to make a roomy bag, leaving some space above the birds. Tuck edges underneath. Roast in the oven preheated to Gas 6/400°F/200°C for 40 minutes, or until cooked through. Serve in the bags so guests can unwrap their parcel, like opening a present.

WINE: White Châteauneuf-du-Pape, New World Chardonnay, or white Dão from Portugal.

Choucroûte Garnie
à L'Alsacienne

Alsace is a lovely part of France. It must be. Nothing untoward has ever happened to me there, even with an enthusiastic taste for the clear fruit brandies the region is famous for.

This is one of the best-known Alsace dishes, though funnily enough, the best I have ever eaten was in one of my favourite restaurants on the Left Bank in Paris.

This is a real rib-tickler, especially on a cold winter's day. It is simple to cook, but doing something energetic while this is happening is recommended.

SERVES 4

1lb/450g jar sauerkraut
2 tbsp oil
1 onion, peeled and sliced
2 cloves garlic, peeled and
    sliced
1 pork knuckle
4 thick slices belly of pork
6 Strasbourg sausages, or
    real *frankfurters*

4oz/100g smoked pork loin,
    thickly sliced
³/₄pt/450ml Alsace Riesling
8 juniper berries
4 coriander seeds
2 cloves
freshly ground black pepper

Empty sauerkraut into a colander and rinse thoroughly to get the pickling liquid out. Reserve.

In a pan, heat oil and gently fry onion and garlic until softened. Remove with a slotted spoon and transfer to a flameproof casserole. Add pork knuckle to pan and brown all over. Add to casserole. Brown belly of pork and sausages in pan and add these as well with smoked pork loin.

Pour over white wine. Add juniper berries, coriander seeds and cloves. Bring to the boil, then turn down and simmer for 30 minutes. Add sauerkraut and season with plenty of freshly ground black pepper. Continue simmering, covered, for about another hour, or until meats are tender. Remove lid for the last 10 minutes of cooking. Serve with boiled potatoes.

WINE: Riesling, preferably from Alsace.

Blanquette de Veau

The switch to nouvelle cuisine, *greater interest in Mediterranean dishes, and the increasing use of Asian herbs and spices in smart cooking has virtually swamped the cooking of France. The use of high cholesterol ingredients is virtually a no-no. But you must make an exception with this dish.*

A simple, traditional country stew with a delicate and creamy taste. Use white pepper to season since the dish is – *very* white. Black pepper makes it look as if it has been made in a gravel pit.

SERVES 4

2lb/900g boned shoulder of
   veal, trimmed and in cubes
1 onion, peeled and roughly
   chopped
1 carrot, peeled and chopped
1 stick celery, chopped
¹/₂pt/300ml light dry white
   wine
³/₄pt/450ml veal or chicken
   stock

salt and freshly ground white
   pepper
bouquet garni
8oz/225g button mushrooms
2 egg yolks
4 tbsp double cream
squeeze lemon juice

Place veal in a pan with onion, carrot and celery. Pour over wine and stock and season with salt and freshly ground white pepper. Add bouquet garni, and bring to bubbling. Remove any scum on the surface with a spoon. Turn down heat and simmer for 1¹/₂ hours, or until veal is tender. Pick out and discard the bouquet garni and vegetables. Add mushrooms to the pan and cook 10 minutes more. Strain cooking liquor from the pan into another pan.

Beat together egg yolks and cream and add a couple of spoonfuls of the hot cooking liquor. Slowly add this mixture to the remainder of the cooking liquor over gentle heat, stirring constantly until sauce thickens. Do not allow it to boil, or the eggs will scramble.

Return veal and mushrooms to the pan. Adjust seasoning and add a squeeze of lemon juice. Serve with noodles.

WINE: Dry white Graves, Alsace Pinot Gris or dry Muscat, California Fumé Blanc, Australian Verdelho.

Spring Casserole

As a cook, I would hardly call myself a chef. I react to the changing of the seasons, but do not over-react. The part of Australia I live in has a very Mediterranean climate, so to rub salt into the wounds of old friends, I would say our winters are about the same as English summers.

When spring arrives it means we are heading for hot weather, so all the winter recipes are put away. It is simply too hot to eat them. Spring also means the arrival of the new season's vegetables, so I use them to cook this simple and tasty dish as a final reminder of winter.

A light fresh-tasting dish of braised lamb chops with small whole spring vegetables, cooked in white wine and stock.

SERVES 4

3 tbsp oil
1 onion, peeled and finely
    chopped
2 cloves garlic, peeled and
    crushed
8 lamb loin chops, trimmed
seasoned flour
8oz/225g baby carrots
8oz/225g tomatoes
    (preferably skinned)

1 tbsp chopped fresh parsley
1/2pt/300ml lamb or chicken
    stock
1/4pt/150ml dry white wine
salt and freshly ground black
    pepper
8oz/225g baby new
    potatoes, scrubbed
12 button onions, peeled
2oz/50g fresh or frozen peas

Heat 2 tbsp oil in a pan and gently fry chopped onion and
garlic until softened. Transfer to an ovenproof casserole.
Dip chops in seasoned flour, then brown in the same pan,
on both sides, using remaining oil. Add to the casserole.
Scrub carrots and trim away root and feathery leaves,
leaving a little stump of leaves still on. Add to casserole.
Chop tomatoes and add these with chopped parsley.

Add 1 more tbsp seasoned flour to the pan and stir
around over low heat for 1 minute. Gradually add stock
and wine, stirring. Add to the casserole. Season with salt
and freshly ground black pepper. Add baby new potatoes
and button onions. Cover, then cook in the preheated
oven at Gas 4/350°F/180°C for an hour. Add peas 15
minutes before the end. Check seasoning before serving.

WINE: I like to drink with this a white wine with a bit of
acidity and zip to it. An inexpensive Chablis, Sauvignon
Blanc, white Rioja, or Tuscan Galestro.

Suffolk Rabbit Stew

Many people think saffron is a North African spice because of its widespread use in dishes like couscous. However, the largest producer of saffron in the world is Spain.

Every spring, the hard brown earth of the plains of La Mancha – where Don Quixote tilted at windmills – is covered with a carpet of tiny mauve flowers. The back-breaking work of picking these flowers of this relative of the crocus plant has to be done at dawn before the fierce heat of the day kills them off. The petals are then removed by hand to reveal the saffron stigmas. Each flower has only three stigmas, and it takes no less than 225,000 to yield just 1lb/450g of saffron.

This is a robust country dish of slowly cooked rabbit flavoured with bacon, garlic, mushrooms, saffron and white wine. If you buy rabbit joints, the legs and saddle are the meatiest.

SERVES 4

6 tbsp oil
4 rashers streaky bacon, rinded and chopped
4oz/100g small button mushrooms, wiped and trimmed
1¹/₂lb/700g rabbit joints
seasoned flour
8 shallots, peeled
1 medium onion, peeled and finely chopped

3 cloves garlic, peeled and crushed
¹/₂pt/300ml dry white wine
¹/₄pt/150ml chicken or vegetable stock
good pinch saffron threads
good squeeze lemon juice
salt and freshly ground black pepper

Heat 2 tbsp oil in a pan and cook bacon until crisp. Transfer to a flameproof casserole. Add mushrooms to the pan and fry 1 minute. Add these to the casserole. Dip rabbit joints in seasoned flour. Add remaining oil to the pan and fry rabbit until browned all over. Transfer to the casserole. Finally add shallots, onion and garlic to the pan and cook until golden. Add these to the other ingredients.

Pour a little wine into the pan and bring to the boil, stirring to scrape up any sediment. Add with remaining wine and stock to the casserole. Add saffron threads. Bring to the boil, then turn down to simmer, covered, for 1 hour. Add lemon juice and check seasoning, then continue simmering until rabbit is tender, about 20 minutes.

WINE: A white or red wine will suit this dish. Try an Australian or Californian Chardonnay for a white, or a decent *cru* Beaujolais for a red.

Chilled Rhubarb Soufflé

When I was a boy, my mother would occasionally serve rhubarb and custard as dessert. I could not stand it, perhaps because of the sharpness of the rhubarb. My father had decreed that his sons could not leave the table until the food was eaten. When tiny voices were raised in complaint, he would mumble on about the Great Depression, which I suppose was fair enough. But it was a little hard to fathom how it applied to us.

When I got to England, where they knew how to cook rhubarb, I began to appreciate its finer points.

This much maligned and slightly unfashionable plant is the base of a surprisingly delicious and delicate creamy dessert, served with a sweet wine sauce.

SERVES 4

2 sticks young rhubarb, trimmed and chopped

3 tbsp caster sugar

4 tbsp water

2 eggs, separated, plus 1 egg yolk

4fl oz/100ml double cream, whipped

1 sachet gelatine dissolved in 3 tbsp boiling water

FOR THE SAUCE

2 sticks young pink rhubarb, trimmed and chopped

1 wine glass sweet white wine

1 tbsp caster sugar

Place rhubarb in a pan with 2 tbsp sugar and the water. Bring to the boil and simmer until rhubarb is soft. Whizz in a blender to make a purée. Reserve and cool.

79

Whisk egg yolks with remaining sugar over very gentle heat until thick and creamy. Remove from heat and stir in cold purée. Fold in whipped cream and stir in gelatine. Whisk egg whites stiff, and carefully fold in. Pour into an oiled mould and leave to set in the fridge.

To make the sauce, poach rhubarb in wine with sugar until soft. Purée and cool. Turn out mould on to a pretty plate, and serve sauce separately.

WINE: A glass of sweet white wine such as Sauternes.

Peaches with Sauternes

Mention of Sauternes always puts me in mind of one of the finest wine tastings I have ever done. It was a joint tasting of two of the world's great sweet wines, the Sauternes of the legendary French producer, Château d'Yquem, and the leading German vineyard, Schloss Vollrads. The tasting was held at the schloss overlooking the Rhine. It was not a look at a few wines from each producer, but a tour de force, with wines going back into the last century and beyond. All were in the pink.

At the end of the tasting most of the guests were given a cellar tour, but a few of us hung back, for there on the tasting table was glass after unfinished glass of wines from the 1820s to the 1840s. Reverently we sipped away, forgetting to spit this time.

For this simple recipe which can be served warm in winter and cold in summer, you don't necessarily need to use Sauternes. Other sweet wines can be substituted like Barsac or Monbazillac. Even one of the sweeter wines from the Loire, like Quarts de Chaume or Bonnezeaux, will do.

SERVES 4

8 ripe peaches   *¹/₂ bottle sweet white wine*

Peel peaches by blanching in boiling water for 2 minutes. The skins will slip off easily. Halve peaches and remove stones. Cut into thick slices. Place in a pan and cover with sweet wine. Bring to the boil and simmer for 2 minutes. Serve warm, or leave to cool and serve chilled.

WINE: A glass of sparkling wine or even a well-chilled Poire William, the water-clear fruit brandy from Alsace.

CHAPTER 3

Champagne and Sparkling Wine

Champagne Onion Soup

The late André Simon, who did so much to educate people about wine and its pleasures through the many books he wrote, his founding of the International Wine & Food Society, the many tastings he conducted, and so much more, loved Champagne.

For many years, André was the British agent for a leading Champagne house, and as a sort of quality control, he would begin his day by drinking a bottle in the morning. As he got older, he cut it down to a half bottle. But it was a habit he maintained till the end of his life.

Today's Thought Police, who insist that drinking wine will seriously damage your health, might care to reflect that André lived to the ripe old age of, I think, ninety-seven.

André would have used Champagne in this recipe, but any good dry sparkling white wine will do.

SERVES 4

2oz/50g butter
4 tbsp oil
3 Spanish onions, peeled and
    thinly sliced
salt and freshly ground black
    pepper
1 tsp sugar
1/2pt/300ml Champagne or
    dry sparkling white wine

1¹/₂pt/900ml chicken stock
4oz/100g Gruyère cheese,
    grated
3 egg yolks
1 tbsp Cognac
2 tbsp port
4 slices French bread,
    toasted

Heat butter and oil in a pan and add sliced onion. Cover and cook gently for 15 minutes. Take the lid off, add a good pinch of salt and sugar and turn up heat. Continue cooking for another 30 minutes, stirring frequently and keeping an eye on the pan, until onions are golden and softened.

Add Champagne and stock and bring to the boil. Cover and simmer for 15 minutes.

Just before serving, add cheese and stir to melt. Remove from heat and cool slightly. Beat egg yolks with Cognac and port and beat into soup vigorously with a fork. Season with salt and freshly ground black pepper.

To serve, place a slice of toasted French bread at the bottom of four soup bowls and pour hot soup over.

WINE: A glass of Amontillado sherry or Sercial Madeira.

Oysters in Champagne

I have never had the passion for oysters that other people have. I can happily pass by the Belon No. 1 and No. 2, and if oysters are an aphrodisiac, they don't seem to work on friends of mine who enjoy them. Anyway, what is the point of trying to get your girlfriend or boyfriend to eat two dozen oysters to turn him or her on, when the more likely result is that they will be sick?

You also have to be careful with oysters. I was touring southern Ireland with a friend when we stopped for a pub lunch. The local publican said we had to try the local Blarney oysters or whatever. My friend who likes oysters agreed. I was more interested in the faggots.

The 'oysters' arrived and they were whoppers. My friend had to cut them up with a knife. He had to pay a fair old whack for them, too. I did not have the heart to tell him, but I know a scallop when I see one.

By the way, did you know, in those parts of Ireland, they play a game around the country lanes which consists of grown men seeing who can take the fewest rolls of a cricket ball to get between A and B, usually a matter of miles. Only the Irish.

I have included this recipe so you can treat your oyster-loving friends.

SERVES 4

24 oysters	1oz/25g chilled butter, in
1/4pt/150ml fish stock	cubes
1 wine glass Champagne	salt and freshly ground white
5 tbsp double cream	pepper

Scoop oysters from shells. Reserve deep shells and discard the flat ones. Place meats and juice in a large shallow pan over low heat until the juice and flesh go white. Remove meats from pan, leaving liquor behind, and keep warm. Pour fish stock into pan with Champagne. Bring to the boil and reduce by half. Stir in cream and whisk in butter bit by bit. Season with salt and freshly ground white pepper. Return oysters to deep shells and pour over a little sauce.

WINE: Carry on with the fizz.

Pheasant in *Cava*

The Spanish gaily used to call their locally made sparkling wines champagna. Naturally the French were fairly testy about this, so when Spain joined the EEC, one of the conditions of entry was that they came up with a different name and got rid of champagna. The name the industry came up with was cava, which is pretty self-explanatory.

The French must have been fairly rattled anyway, as the two biggest Spanish sparkling wine houses, Codorníu and Freix-enet, between them produce as much sparkling wine a year as the entire Champagne industry. (The maturation cellars of Codorníu are so vast that you tour them on a miniature train.)

In this simple pot–roast, the *cava* brings out the flavour of the gamey gravy.

SERVES 4

4 tbsp oil
1 onion, peeled and finely chopped
2 cloves garlic, peeled and crushed
1 carrot, peeled and chopped
1 leek, washed and sliced
2 oven-ready pheasants

1 wine glass cava
1/4pt/150ml chicken stock
2 sprigs fresh thyme
1 tbsp finely chopped fresh parsley
salt and freshly ground black pepper

Heat half the oil in a frying pan and fry onion and garlic until softened but not browned. Transfer to a large ovenproof casserole with a lid. Add carrot and leek to frying pan and toss around for a couple of minutes. Transfer to casserole.

Turn heat up high and add remaining oil. Brown pheasants all over and sit on top of vegetables in casserole. Pour *cava* and stock into frying pan and stir to scrape up any cooking juices. Bring to the boil and pour over pheasant. Add thyme and parsley and season. Cover with a lid and cook in the preheated oven at Gas 3/325°F/160°C for 1½–2 hours or until birds are tender – this depends on the age of the birds.

Lift out pheasants, cover and reserve in a warm place. Place casserole over heat and boil to reduce cooking juices slightly. Check seasoning. Return birds to casserole and serve straight from the pot.

WINE: A robust Chardonnay from California or Australia.

Champagne Granita

In the 1970s, one of London's better-known restaurants was Lacy's, run by the cookery writer, Margaret Costa, whose Four Seasons Cookery Book *is still a classic, and her husband Bill Lacy. Margaret had a cult following among American foodies, and Lacy's was usually packed with Yanks.*

This is one of Margaret's favourite recipes. It is a most invigorating dessert or pick-me-up.

MAKES 2

5oz/150g caster sugar   *2 tbsp lemon juice or to taste*
¹/₂pt/300ml Champagne

Dissolve the sugar in the Champagne over low heat, and simmer for 5 minutes. Cool, then add the lemon juice slowly, tasting to make sure the lemon does not over-whelm the flavour of the Champagne.

Pour the mix into a freezer tray and place in the freezer. Every half an hour, stir the crystals forming on the edges of the freezer tray to the middle. After 2¹/₂–3 hours the mixture will be a mush, what the Italians call granita.

Spoon the mush into tall glasses and top up with Champagne. Serve immediately.

WINE: More Champagne.

Champagne Sorbet

I have had this simple but delicious dish several times at restaurants in the Champagne region, with Champagne producers in attendance, and have often wondered what they must be thinking when they see the product of at least three years' work disappearing into a water ice.

I like making this in the summer as you can drink the remaining Champagne. Any dry sparkling wine will do, though.

SERVES 6

8oz/225g caster sugar
1pt/600ml water

1/2pt/300ml Champagne or dry sparkling white wine
juice of 1 lemon

Place sugar in a pan with water and stir over low heat until sugar has dissolved. Bring to the boil until syrup is reduced to 1/2pt/300ml. Cool and add Champagne and lemon juice. Pour into a freezer tub and place in the freezer turned to its lowest setting.

When the mix begins to freeze, remove from the freezer and beat well. Return to freezer until solid. Serve in scoops in wine glasses.

WINE: Champagne or Asti Spumante.

Black Velvet Ice Cream

For many years my parents used to hold a party on Christmas Day morning, and invariably it spilled over into lunch.

Part of the reason was that the morning tipple was Black Velvet. This is a rather alluring combination of Champagne and Guinness in about equal proportions. My father used to mix it in a jug over cracked ice to keep it well chilled, a tradition I have maintained.

The trouble with Black Velvet is that it sneaks up on you. It is a pretty lethal combination – but it does not seem to be when you are actually consuming it. I can remember little about what happened after those lunches apart from falling asleep.

Used in moderation, Black Velvet is a good hangover cure, as is ice cream. In this recipe you get the best of both worlds.

An unusual ice cream flavoured with Guinness and Champagne.

SERVES 4

2 eggs, separated
2 tbsp caster sugar
2 tbsp Champagne or other
   sparkling white wine

2 tbsp Guinness
1/2pt/300ml double cream

Whisk egg yolks and sugar until pale and creamy. Pour Champagne into Guinness. Add to egg yolk mix. Whip cream thick and fold in until smoothly incorporated. Whisk the whites stiff and carefully fold in. Transfer to a freezer tub and freeze. This ice cream can be served straight from the freezer.

WINE: Champagne.

CHAPTER 4

Sherry

Gazpacho

Gazpacho is supposed to be an Andalusian creation, but I have ordered it in restaurants all over Spain. All I can report is that when making gazpacho, no two chefs seem to do the same thing. I have had it in a restaurant outside Granada where it was served almost as a clear broth, with chopped tomatoes and peppers served on side dishes to add as you wanted. Then I have had it in the north where it came thick and creamy. It is supposed to be served chilled, but I have also had it served warm.

What I think lifts this recipe, as it does many soups, is a serious dash of fino sherry at the last moment.

SERVES 4

2 slices stale white bread, crusts removed
cold water
2lb/900g fresh ripe tomatoes, peeled, seeded and chopped
1 green pepper, seeded and chopped
1 onion, peeled and roughly chopped
1 cucumber, peeled and chopped

2 cloves garlic, peeled and crushed
3 tbsp red wine vinegar
1/2pt/300ml cold chicken or vegetable stock
1/4pt/150ml tomato juice
salt and freshly ground black pepper
1 sherry glass fino sherry

FOR THE GARNISH
1 hard-boiled egg, peeled and finely chopped
1/2 cucumber, diced

1/2 onion, peeled and finely chopped
tiny garlic croûtons

Soak bread in enough cold water to cover. Squeeze out and place in the blender with tomatoes, pepper, onion, cucumber, garlic, vinegar, stock and tomato juice. Whizz until as smooth as possible. Season with salt and freshly ground black pepper. Chill.

Stir sherry into soup and pour into bowls. Serve with garnishes in separate side dishes for diners to add their own.

WINE: Chilled fino sherry or a good rosé wine.

Sherry Tortilla

Sometimes I find myself in unlikely places. I was once on board the Al Andaluz – the Spanish equivalent of the Orient Express – to do a story about it. The destination was Malaga, but I needed to get off beforehand, and take a car to Granada to fly home.

When the train stopped at my remote station, no one was waiting. I was bloody miles from nowhere and with not enough money to take a conventional cab. Fortunately, the station master was an understanding chap who spoke a bit of English, and when I explained my predicament, he said, leave it to him. He made a phone call, and to my relief he said the car was on its way, but would be about 20 minutes. Why not go to the bar next door and have a glass of wine, which I did, plus a slice of tortilla for lunch.

Tortilla is easy to make, and in warm weather if you keep it in the fridge, you can simply cut a slice off to have with a glass of wine as a light snack. This recipe has a drop of dry sherry beaten in with the eggs.

SERVES 4

4 large waxy potatoes,
  peeled
2 tbsp oil
2 large Spanish onions,
  peeled and finely sliced
2oz/50g butter

salt and freshly ground black
  pepper
1 tbsp finely chopped fresh
  parsley
6 eggs
3 tbsp fino sherry

Thinly slice potatoes and cook in lightly salted boiling water until just tender. Drain and reserve. Heat oil in a pan and cook onion slowly over low heat until soft and just caramelising. Remove with a slotted spoon and place on a plate.

Melt butter in a large non-stick frying pan. Remove from heat and layer potatoes and onions in pan, seasoning with salt and freshly ground black pepper and sprinkling with parsley in between each layer. Beat eggs with sherry and pour over. Place over low heat and cook until eggs set in a cake and the underneath is cooked. Place under a preheated grill to set the top. Leave to cool. Slide out of pan on to a serving dish and serve cold in slices.

WINE: White Rioja or Valencia, or chilled fino sherry.

Cheddar Rarebit with Sherry

I used to think that Welsh rarebit was a dish cooked with rabbit until I discovered the delights of the chop house at the Café Royal. To my cost, I also discovered the delights of the cellar, which around the mid 1970s was one of the best in London, and that is saying something.

A Welsh rarebit gave you a chance to carry on with the claret, justification enough to avoid the trifle.

This version of Welsh rarebit, flavoured with sherry instead of the usual beer, makes an excellent snack.

SERVES 4

*8oz/225g mature Cheddar
  cheese, grated*
1 egg, beaten
2 tsp Dijon mustard
2 tbsp double cream
2 tbsp dry sherry, or to taste
dash Worcestershire sauce
dash Tabasco
*salt and freshly ground black
  pepper*
4 slices white bread
*watercress sprigs for
  decoration*

Mix cheese, egg, mustard, cream and sherry together in a large bowl until almost smooth. Add Worcestershire sauce and Tabasco. Season with salt and freshly ground black pepper.

Toast bread then cut off crusts. Spread cheese mixture over toast and grill until browned and bubbling. Serve immediately, decorated with sprigs of fresh watercress.

WINE: Any red wine to suit your wallet or purse.

100

Chicken Livers
in Sherry

Every year, the sherry producers used to hold a harvest festival. The centrepiece of this, apart from the blessing of the first grapes, was a large fair in the park of Jerez, the sherry capital. This went on all night, with rides and other amusements for the kids, lots of little outdoor restaurants serving food and sherry, and other attractions. Each of the large sherry houses had a permanent building in the park which they opened for the fair to entertain visitors.

One night I was invited to the Domecq pavilion. I had a lovely night, and around 3am thought it was time to get some sleep. As I was about to go, they told me to stay as the floorshow was about to start.

In the next two hours I saw some of the finest flamenco dancing and heard some of the finest flamenco music. It was not the sort of thing tourists ever see, a pure expression of Spanish culture, and quite mesmerising.

As I walked back to my hotel, the sun came up. All around me were families going home from the fair. How they ever did any work that day is a complete mystery to me.

A quick snack or hot first course of flash-fried chicken livers cooked with fino sherry and sun-dried tomatoes, served on a thick croûton.

SERVES 4

12oz/350g chicken livers
3 tbsp oil
1 Spanish onion, peeled and finely chopped

2 cloves garlic, peeled and crushed
1 tbsp tomato purée

101

1oz/25g sun-dried tomatoes
   in oil, drained and
   chopped
1/2 wine glass fino sherry

salt and freshly ground black
   pepper
1 tbsp freshly snipped chives
4 large croûtons

Wash chicken livers and pick over to remove any green or gristly bits. Chop into chunks.

Heat 2 tbsp oil in a pan and fry onion and garlic until soft but not browned. Remove with a slotted spoon and reserve. Turn up heat and add remaining oil. Add chicken livers and quickly fry until browned and just cooked through but still pink in the centre. Return onion mix, and stir in tomato purée and sun-dried tomatoes. Pour over sherry and season with salt and freshly ground black pepper. Bring to the boil and simmer for 2 minutes. Sprinkle over chives. Serve immediately on croûtons.

WINE: A southern French red, young Rioja or Chianti, or an inexpensive Merlot if you can find one.

Sweet and Sour Chicken

When I was growing up, my father decided to raise chickens in the back yard. Most people did. They would be called free-range now. On his first attempt to kill a chicken, my father did quite well, initially. He selected a bird, laid its head on the chopping block, grasped it firmly by the legs, and decapitated it. Unfortunately, it jerked so hard that he let go, and the kids were treated to the sight of father haring around, trying to catch a headless chicken.

I prefer to buy them ready-prepared. This oriental-tasting recipe is more about preparation than cooking.

Best made with fresh chicken, this can also be made with leftovers. There are intriguing Eastern flavours with ginger, garlic, chilli and soy in the ingredients, and a lovely balance between sweet and sour with orange juice, sherry, pineapple and vinegar.

SERVES 4

4 boneless chicken fillets, skinned and cut in chunks
salt and freshly ground black pepper
2 egg whites, beaten
2oz/50g cornflour
5 tbsp oil
1 onion, peeled and finely chopped
2 cloves garlic, peeled and crushed
1/2in/1cm fresh ginger, peeled and finely chopped

1 red pepper, seeded and cut into chunks
2 wine glasses dry sherry
1 tbsp tomato purée
2oz/50g sliced fresh pineapple in small pieces (or use canned in own juice, drained)
good dash soy sauce
1 tbsp white wine vinegar
sprig flat parsley for decoration

103

Season chicken chunks. Dip in egg white, then in corn-flour. Heat 3 tbsp oil in a pan and fry all over to crisp, seal and lightly brown.

Heat remaining oil in another pan and gently fry onion, garlic, ginger and pepper until soft but not brown. Pour over sherry and add tomato purée. Bring to bubbling. Add pineapple and browned chicken chunks to the pan. Shake over a good dash of soy and the vinegar. Carry on simmering for 4 minutes, or until chicken and pineapple are cooked through and sauce has thickened slightly. Season with salt and freshly ground black pepper.

Decorate with a sprig of flat parsley and serve with plain rice.

WINE: An inexpensive Chardonnay.

Honey Chicken

In Spain's sherry triangle, they say there is a sherry for every dish, and indeed I have seen it drunk with everything from shark's liver to sweet cakes. It takes a decent steak to put sherry on its back foot.

The fact that the sherry region of Andalucia is also the premier part of Spain for the breeding of fighting bulls means there is a fair amount of steak going round. I have only met the odd sherry producer who will bend the rules and order a bottle of red Rioja with his steak.

This recipe uses a decent dash of cream sherry – a sweet version. This is very easy to prepare, can be served hot or cold, on barbecues or picnics, or just left in the fridge for the kids to snack on.

SERVES 4

8 chicken drumsticks

FOR THE MARINADE
2 tbsp lemon juice
4 tbsp light soy sauce
2 tbsp runny honey
2 tbsp tomato purée

2 tbsp cream sherry
salt and freshly ground black pepper

Mix marinade ingredients together and pour into a large shallow dish. Place drumsticks in the marinade in one layer and baste with the marinade. Leave for at least 1 hour, turning every now and then.

Transfer to a rack in a roasting tin and baste with the marinade. Cook in the preheated oven at Gas 5/375°F/190°C for about 20 minutes, basting, until chicken is cooked through (the juices will run clear), and skin is caramelised and golden.

WINE: Any inexpensive dry white wine.

Sherry Duck

In sherry country, as elsewhere in Spain and much of Latin America, dinner is served disconcertingly late in the eyes of outsiders. At one memorable dinner at a sherry bodega, the main course arrived on the table at 5.30am. Our small party tottered back to the hotel. It would have been churlish to refuse the frequent glasses of sherry that had come our way all night.

It was too late to go to bed as we had a fairly early start. I suggested a swim and a cold beer might get us back into shape for the day to come. Our leader, a former Royal Marine captain, asked a waiter to bring us beers poolside. 'The bar is closed,' said the waiter. Our leader politely led him to the bar, took hold of the wooden partition and with a mighty heave, rolled it up, snapping the locks. 'Now the bloody bar is open,' he said.

The waiter decided life was too short to argue with a man like that, and served the beers.

The Spanish are fond of using ground almonds to thicken stew gravies. In this slow-cooked duck stew, ground almonds work well with a decent splash of sherry to give a delicious result. Use a Barbary duck for this if you can – these have less fat than ordinary ducks.

SERVES 4

2 tbsp oil
1 onion, peeled and finely chopped
3 cloves garlic, peeled and crushed
1 Barbary duck, in 8 pieces

1pt/600ml duck or chicken stock
1 wine glass dry sherry
1 tbsp finely chopped fresh parsley
4 tbsp ground almonds

106

salt and freshly ground black
  pepper
squeeze lemon juice

extra chopped fresh parsley
  to decorate

Heat oil in a pan and fry onion and garlic until soft but not browned. Remove with a slotted spoon and transfer to a deep flameproof casserole. Add duck pieces to frying pan in batches and fry to seal and brown. Transfer to casserole. Pour over stock and sherry and bring to the boil. Add parsley, lower heat, cover and simmer gently for 1½ hours or until duck is tender.

At the end of cooking time, stir in ground almonds. Season with salt, freshly ground black pepper and lemon juice. Sprinkle in some freshly chopped parsley just before serving.

WINE: A zesty wine is needed like a white Rioja, Tuscan Galestro or decent Verdicchio.

Emperor's Turkey

When Christmas or Thanksgiving rolls around, and you are once again contemplating yet another boring roast turkey, you might consider this recipe which will certainly liven the bird up. The stuffing will definitely get your guests talking.

A terrifically different way to cook the traditional bird. This one is stuffed with egg-fried rice, and is basted with an oriental-style mix of five-spice, ginger, brown sugar, soy sauce, sherry and lemon juice for a dark brown crisp glaze.

SERVES 6

8lb/3.6kg oven-ready turkey

FOR THE BASTE
¹/4pt/150ml water
4 tbsp dark brown sugar
3 tbsp soy sauce
3 tbsp oloroso sherry

2 tsp five-spice powder
2 tsp ground ginger
juice of 1 lemon

FOR THE STUFFING
3 tbsp oil
*1 onion, peeled and finely
  chopped*
*4 spring onions, finely
  chopped*
*2 cloves garlic, peeled and
  crushed*
*1in/2.5cm fresh ginger,
  peeled and finely chopped*

*10oz/275g cooked long-grain
  rice (cooked weight)*
*2 tbsp finely chopped fresh
  coriander*
*salt and freshly ground black
  pepper*
*4oz/100g best peeled
  prawns*
2oz/50g butter
2 eggs, beaten

Place turkey on a trivet and pour over boiling water. Leave to dry – this seals the pores and helps the baste to coat the skin.

While this is happening, make the stuffing. Heat oil in a pan and gently fry onion, spring onion, garlic and ginger over low heat until softened. Stir in rice to coat with the spicy mix. Add coriander and season well with salt and lots of freshly ground black pepper. Add prawns and stir. Remove from heat. Melt butter in a pan and scramble eggs until just on the point of setting, but still runny. Stir through stuffing mix. Leave to cool completely.

108

Stuff the neck end of the turkey with the rice mix, and secure the skin flap underneath with a toothpick or small skewer.

Place turkey on a trivet in a roasting tray. Preheat oven to Gas 5/375°F/190°C. Mix baste ingredients together and paint over bird. The baste is liquid – do not worry if it seems thin – this is right.

Keeping your eye on it, cook for 2½ hours (or until the juices run clear when the thigh is pierced with a skewer), painting with the baste every 15 minutes or so. Gradually the skin will darken and crisp. The legs might darken faster than the breast. If this happens, cover them with foil for the rest of the cooking time.

Serve on a warmed platter surrounded with stir-fried vegetables.

WINE: If you can find it, Australian sparkling Shiraz is the perfect match with turkey. Otherwise, select a full-bodied Chardonnay.

Drunken Pork

I have a friend who, when I mention I am cooking a Chinese meal, camps on my doorstep until I let him in. It is not so much that my Peking duck is pretty good, it is just that he does not know anyone else who cooks serious Chinese food at home.

I really became interested in Chinese food when I got to know the London-based expert, Ken Lo, a quite amazing man who played Davis Cup tennis for China before the last war. Whenever I dined at Ken's restaurant, he would come and join my table. Ken's wife, or his doctor, or a combination of both, had ordered Ken to stop smoking. Ken, being Chinese, was a furious smoker, so I always had to have a spare packet on hand so he could have a surreptitious fag or three.

Ken was instrumental in teaching me not to be frightened of cooking Chinese food, though I draw the line at dim sum or yum char.

Thinly sliced pork fillet first marinated, then quickly stir-fried with red pepper, beansprouts and spring onion. A tip with this recipe – to slice the meat finely, semi-freeze it first.

SERVES 4

8oz/225g fillet of pork, thinly sliced into strips
2 tbsp oil
1 in/2.5cm fresh ginger, peeled and cut in thin matchsticks
2 cloves garlic, peeled and crushed

1/2 red pepper, seeded and cut into strips
4 spring onions, trimmed and cut into lengths, then halved lengthways
good shake light soy sauce
2 tbsp dry sherry

4oz/100g beansprouts,
  picked over

salt and freshly ground black
  pepper

FOR THE MARINADE
1 wine glass dry sherry
2 tbsp light soy sauce

2 cloves garlic, peeled and
  crushed

Place marinade ingredients in a bowl and add sliced pork. Turn over in the mix, then cover and leave in the fridge for 30 minutes.

Heat oil in a wok or large pan, and toss ginger, garlic, red pepper and spring onions around for 1 minute. Add pork and quickly stir-fry this until it stiffens. Still over high heat, add soy sauce and sherry and cook 1 minute more. Add beansprouts and cook another minute until they are heated through but still crisp. Season before serving.

WINE: This recipe calls for a flavoursome Australian Chardonnay.

Tang Ton Lamb and Leeks

Lamb seems to be the missing ingredient in most Chinese cooking. And you rarely see it on the menus in Chinese restaurants. Why this is, I don't know. Perhaps the Chinese make lousy shepherds.

Anyway, living in a country with serious futures in sheep, this fast and flavourful recipe remains on the books.

An oriental-style dish of tender lamb fillet cooked with leeks and chilli in sherry and richly flavoured oyster sauce.

SERVES 4

4 tbsp oil
1 onion, peeled, halved and
    sliced
2 cloves garlic, peeled and
    crushed
1 green chilli, seeded and
    finely chopped

2 thin leeks, trimmed,
    washed and thinly sliced
    diagonally
1lb/450g lamb fillet, thinly
    sliced
4 tbsp dry sherry
3 tbsp oyster sauce
salt and freshly ground black
    pepper

Heat half the oil in a pan and add onion, garlic and chilli. Fry over gentle heat until soft but not brown. Remove with a slotted spoon and reserve. Add leeks and cook these for about 3 minutes. Remove and reserve with onion mix.

Turn up heat to high, and add remaining oil. Stir-fry lamb slices in batches to seal and brown. Return vegetables to pan and pour over sherry and oyster sauce.

112

Toss to coat and bring briefly to the boil. Season with salt and freshly ground black pepper, and serve immediately.

WINE: Dry rosé or Australian Riesling.

Carrots in Amontillado

Amontillado is an aged fino sherry which gradually acquires different characteristics from the dry tangy fino as it matures in cask. Amontillado is basically a shade sweeter, with an interesting aroma of hazelnuts.

You can smell the hazelnuts as you cook this dish. Amontillado has a special affinity with the nutty sweetness of carrots.

SERVES 4

*1lb/450g carrots, peeled and
   cut in sticks
chicken stock or water
1¹/₂oz/40g butter*

*3 tbsp amontillado sherry
salt and freshly ground black
   pepper
1 tbsp freshly snipped chives*

Cook carrots in stock or boiling salted water to cover until just tender. Drain.

Melt butter in a pan and add carrots. Toss around for 1 minute. Add sherry and simmer until it has practically disappeared. Season with salt and freshly ground black pepper. Stir in freshly snipped chives. Transfer to a serving dish and pour buttery juices over.

WINE: Depends on the main course.

Salad Emilia

It was the Italians and Spanish who gave me a proper appreciation of ham, the Italians with Parma, the Spanish with Serrano and, latterly, the much rarer Jabugo. The Spanish swear by Jabugo, which comes from pigs who dine mainly on acorns and, I was told, the odd snake, which is why Jabugo has its fine flavour. I cannot vouch for the snake bit though.

Colourful and filling Parma ham salad in a dry sherry dressing.

SERVES 4

8oz/225g baby new potatoes, scrubbed
8oz/225g baby carrots, trimmed and scrubbed
8oz/225g broccoli florets

2 courgettes, trimmed and in strips
8 wafer-thin slices Parma ham
1 medium Spanish onion, peeled and finely chopped

FOR THE DRESSING
1 tbsp sherry vinegar
1 tbsp dry sherry
1 tsp Dijon mustard
4 tbsp sunflower oil

1 tbsp freshly snipped chives
salt and freshly ground black pepper

Cook potatoes and baby carrots in boiling salted water. Blanch broccoli florets and courgette strips. While the vegetables are still warm, heap all this into a bowl with ham and chopped onion.

Beat vinegar and sherry into mustard, then gradually add oil. Stir in chives, then season with salt and freshly

115

ground black pepper. Pour over salad and toss through. Serve immediately, while the vegetables are still warm.

WINE: White Rioja, or Galestro from Tuscany.

Sweet Potato Pudding

The recipe for this unusual dessert I picked up during a visit to Cape Town. I suspect it has Cape Malay origins.

A sustaining and filling pudding made with mashed sweet potatoes and flavoured with sweet sherry.

SERVES 4

1 sweet potato, peeled and
 cut into chunks
4oz/100g butter
2oz/50g caster sugar
1 tsp ground cinnamon

good grating fresh nutmeg
4 tbsp sweet sherry
3 eggs, separated
icing sugar for dusting

Boil potato, drain well and mash. Cream butter and sugar until light and fluffy. Beat in mashed sweet potato, cinnamon, nutmeg and sherry. Beat egg yolks and then vigorously stir into mixture with a wooden spoon until everything is well blended.

Whisk egg whites until stiff peaks are formed. Fold into potato mix with a metal spoon. Spoon into an ovenproof dish and smooth surface. Bake in the pre-heated oven at Gas 6/400°F/200°C for 30 minutes or until firm. Dust with icing sugar and serve with custard.

WINE: Any wine made from Muscat grapes which is not bone dry – Muscat de Beaumes de Venise, for example.

Orgasmic Trifle

My maternal grandmother used to smoke furiously and enjoy a serious tipple or two each day, so I guess it's in my genes.

One of the desserts my mother would occasionally knock up was a trifle, to which she would always add a decent dash of sherry. She could never figure out why she had to go and buy a new bottle because so little was left in the old. It was Gran, who always had a thing about trifles . . .

This trifle recipe has puréed apricots on sherry-soaked sponge and marvellous cheat's custard. Simply use instant custard enriched with whipped double cream, and they will never know the difference.

SERVES 6

1 packet trifle sponges
5 tbsp sweet sherry, or to
    taste
2 × 14oz/400g tins apricot
    halves, drained

1 packet instant custard
1/4pt/150ml double cream
3/4pt/450ml whipping cream
1oz/25g flaked almonds

Place a neat layer of sponge in the base of a glass trifle bowl. You may need to break them to fit. Pour over sherry and leave to soak in. Purée apricots and spoon over sponge.

Now for the custard. Make up the instant custard with half the amount of water stated on the packet. Cool, then stir in double cream. Carefully pour over apricots. Leave to cool completely, then chill in the fridge.

Just before serving whip whipping cream and spoon over custard, then smooth surface. Toast almond flakes, cool, then scatter over the top.

WINE: A glass or two of sparkling *cava* wine from Spain, or an inexpensive Australian sparkler.

Peter Langan's Hangover Cure

The late Peter Langan, founder of the eponymous Langan's Brasserie with Michael Caine, was the one person who desperately needed a hangover cure. As a drinker, Langan had a reputation probably only rivalled by that of Oliver Reed.

I was eating at Langan's one day. It was lunchtime and Langan was at the next table drinking Champagne. He was seriously gone, and eventually he crashed off his chair into the aisle, out cold. The waiters simply stepped over him and continued to serve lunch. I have included this recipe for those who have occasion to need it.

I cannot vouch for this, as either I don't have a hangover, or else I am near death and nothing would work. You need a large sealable jar.

12oz/350g pack ready-to-use dried apricots   *1 bottle dry oloroso sherry*

Place apricots in the jar up to halfway, packed in tightly. Cover with sherry. Seal and store in the fridge for three months before using.

WINE: You must be joking!

CHAPTER 5

Port, Madeira and Marsala

Potted Roquefort

The Roquefort industry in the south of France is quite amazing, as it is based around a series of natural caves in which the cheeses pick up the blue veins and mature. You could drive right past without knowing you were at the home of one of the most aristocratic cheeses.

Make this simple, but tasty snack when you have a spare moment and slip it in the fridge for later.

SERVES 4

4oz/100g cream cheese　　　*freshly ground black pepper*
1 tbsp tawny port　　　　　*4oz/100g Roquefort cheese*
squeeze lemon juice

Mash cream cheese with port and lemon juice. Season with plenty of freshly ground black pepper. Crumble Roquefort and stir into cream cheese mix. Pack into a pot and chill before serving.

WINE: For lunch, try one of the zippy new white wines from Trentino Alto Adige in the Italian Alps. For a late-night snack, have a glass of tawny port.

Potted Stilton and Port

I never have any trouble sleeping, and once my head is down it is quite difficult to wake me. I have slept through hurricanes, earthquakes and other natural disasters, and a few man-made ones too.

Once in the Douro, after a long session on the port, I retired to my bed. Two of the others at table decided it would be singularly amusing to place two or three chickens in my room. I blame it on the port. They duly did so, thinking the chickens

124

would arouse me. They did not. The next morning, one of the two came in and asked if I had any unusual experiences during the night. Rather perplexed, I said I had not. Then came a cackle from under the spare bed, and when we investigated we found three very frightened chickens that had made a frightful mess on the floor.

I had the pleasure of having my morning cup of tea in bed while watching my friend clean up the mess on his hands and knees.

A classic combination, this simple recipe makes a perfect late-night snack.

SERVES 4

12oz/350g Stilton cheese	freshly ground black pepper
3 tbsp port	brown toast, crusts removed,
squeeze lemon juice	for serving

Mash Stilton with a fork. Mash in port and lemon juice. Season with freshly ground black pepper.

Spoon mix into a pot and smooth surface. Chill in the fridge for 30 minutes. Serve with brown toast.

WINE: A glass of tawny port.

Sole Fillets in
White Port with Grapes

The Douro Valley in northern Portugal, home of port, is one of the loveliest and most unspoiled parts of Europe. Little has changed there except the damming of the river itself, which put paid to the historic boat race in special boats called barcos. *Few tourists get to the upper Douro, for the simple reason there is nowhere to stay, and it is too far to do in a day from Oporto on the coast. The only way you can visit for any length of time is if one of the port houses invites you to stay in one of their lodges.*

Most people think of port as being red in colour, but in the Douro the preferred aperitif is chilled white port, and plenty of it. The trouble is that you cannot comprehend you are drinking something as strong as red port, and it can be a lethal drink, particularly allowing for the cumulative effect of red port later.

I once watched a senior British wine buyer nearly drown as it all became too much for him and he fell sound asleep at the dining table. Unfortunately his head was heading towards a large bowl of soup in front of him. A neighbour quietly guided his head to one side.

Classy dinner party dish of sole with green grapes, spiked with white port.

SERVES 4

1oz/25g butter	4 Dover soles, filleted and
4 shallots, peeled and finely	skinned
chopped	1 egg yolk
1/2pt/300ml fish stock	5 tbsp double cream

126

4oz/100g seedless green
  grapes, halved
3 tbsp white port

salt and freshly ground white
  pepper
snipped fresh chives for
  decoration

Melt butter in a pan and fry shallots until soft but not brown. Pour in fish stock and bring to the boil. Add sole fillets, turn down heat and poach gently, covered, for 5 minutes or until fish is cooked through. Lift out fillets with a fish slice and place on a plate. Cover and keep hot.

Reduce fish stock by a third by bubbling rapidly over high heat. Beat egg yolk with cream. Remove pan from heat and whisk in egg yolk mixture. Add grapes. Return to low heat and stir until thickened but do not allow to boil. Stir in white port then season with salt and freshly ground white pepper.

Arrange sole fillets on individual plates and spoon sauce and grapes over. Sprinkle with snipped chives for decoration.

WINE: A reasonable white Burgundy or New World Chardonnay.

Sauce Madère

I am pleased to report that the quality Madeiras are slowly returning to fashion after nearly giving up the ghost. Madeira seemed to have become the preserve of restaurant kitchens where it is used for sauces.

I would buy a very good bottle of Madeira as this recipe does not call for much – and you can drink the rest at leisure.

This sauce makes an excellent alternative to gravy to go with roast beef (see page 32). Also good with venison, or duck.

Serves 6

3 rashers streaky bacon,
   rinded and diced
2oz/50g butter
1 carrot, peeled and diced
2 sticks celery, finely
   chopped
1 small onion, peeled and
   finely chopped

2oz/50g plain flour
1pt/600ml beef stock
1 tbsp tomato purée
1 tsp dried oregano
6fl oz/175ml Madeira
salt and freshly ground black
   pepper

Put bacon in a non-stick pan and cook gently until the fat runs. Add butter and melt it, then add vegetables. Cook these over low heat for 10 minutes, until softened. Add flour and stir over low heat for 1 minute. Stirring, gradually add beef stock, tomato purée and oregano. Bring to the boil, then simmer, stirring, until sauce is thick. Strain and reserve.

Meanwhile pour 5floz/150ml Madeira into a pan and reduce to 2 tablespoons. Stir this into the reserved sauce and season to taste with salt and freshly ground black pepper. Add remaining Madeira little by little, to taste. Pour into a sauce boat and serve.

WINE: Depends on what it is served with.

Zabaglione

The key ingredient of zabaglione (or zabaione as I think it should be spelt) is Marsala, the classic Italian dessert wine that has now been largely relegated to the kitchen.

Marsala was first created by the Englishman John Woodhouse on Sicily in 1773 as a rival to sherry and port. Admiral Horatio Nelson helped popularise it by provisioning his navy with the wine while campaigning off Sicily. When the Italian patriot Garibaldi landed with his famous 'Thousand' to free Italy, he adopted the local product, Marsala. 'This is a strong and generous wine like the people who produce it, like the men who fight with me for freedom. Here is a wine which will make its name in history.'

Garibaldi only got it partly right. Marsala enjoyed a flurry of popularity in the Victorian era, but then faded from view into the kitchens of Italian restaurants.

This dessert requires patience to make but will bring rewards.

SERVES 4

6 egg yolks

3oz/75g caster sugar

¼pt/150ml Marsala

dessert biscuits to serve

Beat egg yolks with sugar and Marsala in a bowl. Place bowl over a pan of simmering water over low heat. Whisk continuously until mix is thickened and frothy. Remove whisk, and if it leaves a trail, the zabaglione is ready. Pour into glasses and serve with dessert biscuits for dipping.

WINE: The Italian Vinsanto or a glass of Asti Spumante.

CHAPTER 6

Pastis and Vermouth

Potted Prawns

Coming from Australia, I thought I was reasonably well up on prawns, which we have in abundance, and in my childhood even caught them myself in the river. The simplest way was for two of us to drag a net at night using a kerosene lantern to attract the prawns. They were then boiled in a drum on the beach and eaten straightaway. During the day, you could catch them by hand by going to a rocky area and groping around the base of the rocks where they had settled into the sand.

I was even aware that prawns came in different sizes, but was knocked out one day when I visited a café at Puerto Santa Maria, the old port of the sherry industry. Apart from the odd crab, the café sold nothing but prawns, and they must have had at least two dozen different varieties on sale. It was difficult to know where to begin.

Best peeled prawns flavoured with vermouth and set in spiced butter.

SERVES 4

6oz/175g unsalted butter
salt and freshly ground black
  pepper
2 tsp cayenne pepper

12oz/350g best peeled
  prawns
4 tsp white vermouth

Melt butter over gentle heat and season. Add cayenne. Divide prawns between four ramekins. Sprinkle over vermouth. Pour over butter to cover. Leave in the fridge until set. To serve, turn out on small serving plates and serve with brown toast.

WINE: I would drink a chilled fino sherry with this dish, but any inexpensive dry white wine will do.

Cold Sea Bass with Noilly Prat Mayonnaise

When you say vermouth, most people think of Italy, and the vast businesses that Martini and Cinzano have built around Milan and Turin. However the French also have a vermouth industry, and the best-known producer is Noilly Prat. I have always found Noilly to be slightly fuller bodied and more herby than the Italian vermouths, which is why I use it to spike the mayonnaise in this dish.

A good summer buffet dish served with the luxurious sea bass, this mayonnaise is also an excellent foil for cold salmon.

3lb/1.4kg sea bass, cleaned, head on
2 spring onions, trimmed and chopped

salt and freshly ground black pepper
1 tbsp Noilly Prat
cucumber slices to garnish

FOR THE MAYONNAISE
1 tsp Dijon mustard
1 egg yolk
1/4pt/150ml sunflower oil
1 tbsp Noilly Prat

good squirt lime juice
zest of 1/2 lime
freshly ground white pepper

Lay a large sheet of foil on a work top and place the bass in the middle. Sprinkle over spring onions, salt and freshly ground black pepper, and Noilly Prat. Loosely wrap fish and cook in the preheated oven at Gas 4/350°F/180°C for 20 minutes, or until tender.

Remove from oven and transfer to a work top. Remove foil, peel off skin and discard. Transfer fish to a serving platter and leave to cool.

For the mayonnaise, first spoon mustard into a bowl and add egg yolk. With an electric whisk running, gradually add the oil, drip by drip, beating it all in before adding any more. When the mixture visibly begins to thicken you can relax slightly and add oil in a thin stream but still whisking in. When all oil is incorporated, stir in Noilly Prat, a squirt of lime juice and the lime zest. Season with salt and freshly ground white pepper.

Decorate bass with a ruff of overlapping blanched cucumber slices. Serve with mayonnaise in a separate bowl.

WINE: This is the dish which calls for the opening of a good white Burgundy. Chablis, Sancerre or Muscadet would also be fine.

Pork and Ginger Stew
with Apricots

Ginger comes from tropical Asia, and gets its name from the Sanskrit word sringavera, *meaning 'horn root', an allusion to its appearance. It is one of the most versatile of the natural flavourings, and is used in everything from chutneys to curries and stews, biscuits and preserves, even ice cream.*

Waverley Root in his excellent book, Food, *says that Queen Elizabeth (the first, that is) created the gingerbread man when she ordered the court baker to make little cakes in the images of her courtiers.*

Vermouth is the booze in this exotic pork dish.

SERVES 4

1¹/₂lb/700g lean pork, in
  cubes
seasoned flour
3 tbsp sunflower oil
8 shallots, peeled and
  chopped
2 tsp finely chopped fresh
  ginger
2 cloves garlic, peeled and
  crushed

¹/₂ wine glass vermouth
1 tbsp tomato purée
³/₄pt/450ml chicken stock
1 tbsp finely chopped fresh
  coriander
8 ready-to-use dried apricots
salt and freshly ground black
  pepper
extra chopped coriander for
  decoration

Dip pork in seasoned flour. Fry in hot oil in batches, until browned. Transfer to a flameproof casserole. Add shallots, ginger and garlic to pan. Cook over gentle heat until softened. Add vermouth, tomato purée, chicken stock and coriander. Bring back to bubbling and pour over

pork. Add apricots and seasoning. Cover and simmer for
1¹/₂ hours, or until pork is tender. Sprinkle over extra
chopped coriander before serving.

WINE: Cape Chenin Blanc, New Zealand or Chilean
Chardonnay.

Pork with Leeks

*The dry vermouth used in this recipe has its origins in the
distant past: the ancient Greeks and Romans used to add herbs
to wine for medicinal reasons, and also to help disguise bad or
harsh wine. The modern patent vermouths were developed in
the late eighteenth century with Antonio Carpano of Turin
given most of the credit. To a white wine base is added sugar
syrup and more than fifty herbs and other flavourings such as
hyssop, calamus root, forget-me-not, blessed thistle and hore-
hound.*

Slow cooking of this results in a delicate herby pork dish
lightly flavoured with sage, enhanced by vermouth.

SERVES 4

1¹/₂lb/700g lean pork, in
  cubes
seasoned flour
4 tbsp oil
4 medium leeks, trimmed,
  washed and cut in 1 in/
  2.5cm lengths
3 tbsp vermouth

¹/₂pt/300ml pork or chicken
  stock
1 tsp finely chopped fresh
  sage leaves
3 tbsp double cream
salt and freshly ground black
  pepper

Dip pork cubes in seasoned flour. Heat 2 tbsp oil in a pan and fry meat in batches to brown. Place in a flameproof casserole. Add remaining oil to pan and fry leeks for a couple of minutes. Add to casserole. Pour over vermouth and stock. Add sage. Bring to bubbling, then turn down to simmer. Cover and cook for 1¹/₂ hours, or until pork is tender. Remove lid and add cream and stir in. Season with salt and freshly ground black pepper.

WINE: Needs a white wine with flavour and body like an Australian Chardonnay.

Celery Braised in Vermouth

I once paid a visit to the headquarters and museum of Martini Vermouth. I wanted to know what the main ingredients were, and the man showing me around flatly refused to name any of them except wine. Well, I knew that. As I was being shown around the production plant there were drums and sacks of ingredients with the names neatly stencilled on the side. Why there was all the secrecy when any fool with a pair of eyes could see what was going into the stuff is beyond me. Apparently the secret is in the proportions used, and this information is kept under lock and key.

Martini works very well with celery in this recipe.

SERVES 4

2 heads celery
softened butter
1/2pt/300ml chicken stock
3 tbsp Dry Martini

1 tbsp freshly snipped chives
salt and freshly ground black pepper

Trim celery and cut into 3in/7.5cm strips. Lay in a buttered ovenproof dish. Pour over chicken stock and Martini. Sprinkle over chives. Season with salt and freshly ground black pepper. Cover with foil and cook in the preheated oven at Gas 4/350°F/180°C for 40 minutes, or until celery is tender.

WINE: This will probably be served as a side dish, so it depends on what the main course is. But if you are serving it as a snack or light lunch, try Verdicchio or Soave.

Braised Fennel with Pernod

The parent of Pernod is a drink called absinthe. This drink was first created in 1792 by the Frenchman, Dr Pierre Ordinaire. He saw it as a medical digestif for his patients. However, another Frenchman got hold of the recipe and began manufacturing absinthe commercially. By the 1890s, it was the drink of café society, and had a reputation as an aphrodisiac. However, it contained an ingredient called wormwood, which made absinthe highly addictive. It could kill heavy imbibers.

Forces began to rally against absinthe and when in 1905, a peasant farmer shot his pregnant wife and children, he blamed the drink. Calls were heard from all quarters for its banning. However, the French authorities could not bring themselves to do it. It took the horrifying losses of French lives at the beginning of the First World War (when many soldiers carried absinthe in their canteens instead of water) to bring about the final outlawing of absinthe in 1915.

Pernod, on the other hand, uses the completely non-life-threatening anise as its main flavouring agent.

A way of cooking fennel flavoured with caraway seeds and Pernod. This makes a delicious light supper dish, topped with grated cheese.

SERVES 4

2 bulbs fennel
2 tbsp oil
1/2 onion, peeled and finely
    chopped
1/2pt/300ml vegetable stock

2 tbsp Pernod
1 tsp caraway seeds
salt
8 black peppercorns, bruised
3 tbsp double cream

Scrub and trim fennel and slice. Heat oil in a heavy-bottomed pan and fry onion over gentle heat until soft. Place fennel in pan and pour over stock and Pernod. Sprinkle over caraway seeds, salt and peppercorns. Cover with a lid, then braise for 20 minutes, or until fennel is tender. Remove with a slotted spoon and transfer to a warmed serving plate. Reduce cooking liquid by half and add cream. Bring back to bubbling, then strain and pour over fennel.

WINE: A dry white wine like Soave or Frascati, or a Cape Chenin Blanc.

CHAPTER 7

Beer

Fish in Lager Batter

When I was at school, some of the more devoted mothers opened a tuck shop, which saved a lot of parents, including mine, the hassle of making sandwiches and packing lunch boxes.

However, the girls were not all that devoted, and the tuck shop did not open on Fridays. So the weekly treat was being given enough money to have fish and chips for lunch. We used to race to the fish and chip shop, which was presided over by a large man who seemed to be embalmed in frying fat. However his fish and chips were delicious. I have remained loyal to this gastronomic relic ever since.

This is a crisp and delicious, foolproof batter.

SERVES 4

4 haddock fillets
flour for dusting

oil for deep-frying

FOR THE BATTER
4oz/100g plain flour
1¹/₂tsp baking powder
6 fl oz/175ml lager

salt and freshly ground black
pepper

Place batter flour and baking powder in bowl and gradually beat in lager until you have a consistency of single cream. It should just coat the back of a wooden spoon. Season with salt and freshly ground black pepper.

Dust fish in flour and shake off excess. Dip in batter until coated both sides. Deep-fry in hot oil until crisp and crackly. Drain on kitchen paper. Serve with chips.

WINE: Any inexpensive dry white wine, though I think the faintly salty Frascati goes particularly well.

Belgian Beef and Beer Stew

Several times I have driven through Belgium on the way to, or on the way back from, Italy. Brussels may be the capital of the European Community, but I think its road planners have fixed things so that no one can get out. The ring road around Brussels is entirely devoid of signs telling you how to go anywhere but into the city, and on more than one occasion, I have lapped it several times in total frustration.

The road system has not endeared the Belgians to me, but this hearty dish has.

SERVES 4

2lb/900g chuck steak, trimmed and cut in cubes
seasoned flour
3 tbsp oil
2 onions, peeled and thinly sliced
2 cloves garlic, peeled and crushed
1 level tbsp dark brown sugar

1 fresh bouquet garni (including thyme, parsley, and bay leaf)
1/4pt/150ml beef stock
3/4pt/450ml dark beer (not lager)
salt and freshly ground black pepper
1 tbsp white wine vinegar
1 tbsp finely chopped fresh parsley, for decoration

Dip meat in seasoned flour and shake off excess. Heat oil in a heavy-bottomed flameproof casserole, and fry the meat a few pieces at a time to brown. Remove with a slotted spoon and reserve. Add onion and garlic to the casserole and cook over gentle heat until golden. Return meat to the casserole and sprinkle over sugar. Add bouquet garni. Pour over stock and beer.

Bring to bubbling, then turn down heat to simmer. Cover and cook for 2 hours or until beef is tender. Season and stir in vinegar. Sprinkle with chopped parsley to serve.

WINE: A red with some depth. Reserva Rioja or a red from Ribera del Duero in Spain, a Zinfandel, or Cape Pinotage.

Oxtail with Mushrooms and Chestnuts in Guinness

I once visited Dublin with an Australian friend who had never been there. Big Bob had a powerful thirst on, and he couldn't wait to sink his first pint of the black stuff.

We adjourned to a nearby hostelry and I ordered two pints. The barman poured them and set the glasses down to let the head settle before topping them up. There was a gasp of horror along the bar when Bob's hand snaked out to take the glass. A local took him aside and told him it was the barman who decided when it was ready to drink, not Bob, and a breakdown in diplomatic relations between Ireland and Australia was averted.

Bob enjoyed himself so much that, later on in the day, he called an Irish friend in Australia as another pint was being poured, just to tell him where he was and to make some choice remarks about his Irish ancestry.

This hearty winter dish is simple to make, and, dare I say it, packed with Goodness. Make it the day before, so you can skim off any fat before re-heating.

SERVES 4

2¹/₂lb/1.1kg oxtail, in pieces
seasoned flour
5 tbsp oil
1 Spanish onion, peeled and roughly chopped
2 cloves garlic, peeled and crushed
1 tbsp finely chopped fresh parsley
2 sprigs thyme, chopped
1 bay leaf

¹/₂pt/300ml Guinness
¹/₂pt/300ml beef stock
8oz/225g field mushrooms, wiped and thickly sliced
8oz/225g cooked chestnuts, canned and drained, or vacuum-packed
salt and freshly ground black pepper
extra chopped parsley for decoration

Dip oxtail in seasoned flour and shake off excess. Heat 3 tbsp oil in a pan and fry oxtail pieces until browned. Remove with a slotted spoon and transfer to a flameproof casserole.

Add remaining oil to pan and fry onion and garlic over low heat until softened. Add to casserole with herbs. Pour over Guinness and stock and bring to the boil. Cover casserole with a lid and turn down heat. Simmer for at least 4 hours, making sure the liquid is barely bubbling, until oxtail is tender. Keep an eye on it, adding extra stock if necessary.

Add mushrooms and chestnuts 20 minutes before end of cooking time. Season with salt and freshly ground black pepper. Sprinkle with chopped fresh parsley to serve.

WINE: Well, you can drink stout with it, but I would go for a hearty red wine like a Côtes du Rhône or Australian Shiraz.

Beef and Guinness Pie

Guinness is a stout, but it is a direct descendant of a once popular beer called porter. Porter was first brewed in Shoreditch, East London, in 1722. Some say it got its name from its popularity amongst the porters at the London markets.

Porter successfully crossed to Ireland, where a leading brewer was the Guinness company, but it gradually lost its popularity to the slightly fuller, slightly more bitter version, stout. The last glasses of porter were lifted in 1973, two and a half centuries after it first appeared, and they were appropriately hoisted at a wake in Dublin. Porter still had its fans.

A hearty winter dish with a rich, dark gravy which owes much of its flavour to the son of porter. This processor pastry is the crispest and lightest imaginable, but you can substitute puff or shortcrust.

SERVES 6

4 tbsp oil
1 onion, peeled and finely
  chopped
2 cloves garlic, peeled and
  crushed
2lb/900g chuck steak,
  trimmed and in cubes
seasoned flour
8oz/225g flat mushrooms,
  wiped and sliced

1/2pt/300ml Guinness
1/2pt/300ml beef stock
1 sprig fresh thyme
1 tbsp finely chopped fresh
  parsley
salt and freshly ground black
  pepper
beaten egg to glaze pastry

FOR THE PASTRY
6oz/175g plain flour
4oz/100g unsalted butter

pinch salt
1 egg

First make the pastry. Place flour, butter, salt and egg in the processor and whizz until it forms a ball. Wrap in cling film and leave to chill in the fridge for 30 minutes.

Heat 2 tbsp oil in a pan and fry onion and garlic over gentle heat until soft but not brown. Remove with a slotted spoon and transfer to a flameproof casserole. Toss meat in seasoned flour. Add remaining oil to the pan and fry meat in batches to seal and brown. Do not crowd the pan. Add to casserole. Toss mushrooms around in the pan briefly, then add to casserole. Pour Guinness and stock into pan and bring to the boil, stirring to scrape up any sediment in the pan. Pour over meat, and add thyme and parsley. Season with salt and freshly ground black pepper. Bring to the boil, then immediately turn down to simmer for 1 1/2 hours, or until meat is tender. Cool, then transfer to an oval pie dish.

Roll pastry out on a floured work top. Cut a strip to fit

the rim of the pie dish. Attach it to the rim with water. Place remaining pastry on top of meat and pastry strip, and trim to fit the dish. Use pastry scraps to make decorations. Attach with beaten egg. Brush top of pie with egg to glaze. Bake in the preheated oven at Gas 5/375°F/190°C for 30 minutes, or until pastry is golden and crisp.

DRINKS: You can carry on with the Guinness theme, but I would rather have a chunky red wine that does not hurt the pocket.

Lancashire Hot Pot

My father used to dabble in home brewing – a practice he was forced to stop. We had a very large mulberry tree in the back garden, and apart from beer, my father used to make mulberry wine, though he was the only one brave enough to drink it. He used to lay his home brews down to mature in his workshop. One hot day, when he was away sailing, my mother heard a faint explosion coming from the workshop, followed by a whole series of them. One of his bottles of mulberry wine had exploded in the heat, setting off a chain reaction, and everything was covered in purple mulberry juice.

As my father also restored some quite valuable antique furniture, my mother had to spend a hot and very uncomfortable couple of hours cleaning up the mess. When my father breezed in later that night, he got a right ticking off, and home brewing was banned from our household for ever more.

A traditional dish of meltingly tender neck of lamb and onions, cooked in ale, with a golden roof-tile potato topping.

SERVES 4

3 tbsp oil
1 onion, peeled and thinly sliced
12 neck of lamb chops
seasoned flour
2 large potatoes, peeled and thinly sliced
2 tsp fresh thyme, chopped
salt and freshly ground black pepper
1pt/600ml lamb stock
1/2pt/300ml light ale
1oz/25g butter
1 tbsp freshly snipped chives, for decoration

Heat oil in a pan and fry onion until softened. Remove with a slotted spoon and reserve. Trim neck of lamb chops to remove excess fat, and dip in seasoned flour. Shake off excess and fry in batches over high heat until browned. Layer lamb, onion, and potatoes in a tall earthenware casserole dish, seasoning in between with thyme, salt and freshly ground black pepper. Reserve some neat potato slices for the top. Pour over stock and ale and arrange reserved potatoes in a roof-tile pattern on top. Dot with butter. Bake in the preheated oven at Gas 3/325°F/160°C for 2 hours or until meat is tender and potato topping is golden. Turn up heat to Gas 5/375°F/ 190°C for 10 minutes at the end of cooking if the potatoes are not brown enough. Sprinkle with chives to serve.

WINE: A hearty red like a Châteauneuf-du-Pape, Ribera del Duero, or a red wine from Sicily.

Lamb with Leeks and Lager

The Welsh are a funny people. I once went for a long weekend at a fairly up-market country hotel. On Sunday, I decided to have a gin and tonic before lunch, only to be told that no alcohol was served on Sunday. Against the laws.

However, I was told that if I wandered to the pub down the road, I could get a drink there. How come? I asked. It is across the county line and they are wet, was the reply . . . Also you have to be a little suss about a people who have a leek as their national symbol.

This dish uses the national symbol with lean lamb cooked in lager, which gives the gravy a light, refreshing taste.

SERVES 4

3 tbsp oil
1 Spanish onion, peeled and
  finely chopped
2 large leeks, trimmed, sliced
  and washed
2lb/900g lean lamb, trimmed
  and cut in chunks
seasoned flour

1 × 330ml bottle lager
1/2pt/300ml lamb stock
2 tbsp finely chopped fresh
  parsley
salt and freshly ground black
  pepper
extra chopped parsley for
  decoration

Heat oil in a pan and fry onion until soft but not brown. Add leeks and cook for a further 2 minutes. Remove from pan with a slotted spoon and transfer to a flameproof casserole with a lid. Dip lamb in seasoned flour and fry to seal and brown. Place in casserole. Pour over lager and stock and bring to bubbling.

Sprinkle in parsley and season with salt and freshly ground black pepper.

Cover and simmer for 1¹/₂ hours or until meat is tender. Check seasoning and sprinkle with extra parsley to serve.

Wine: A young Bordeaux, or Chianti Classico.

CHAPTER 8

Cider

Cod and Cider Stew

One of the virtues attributed to cider in past centuries was that it contributed to longevity. In 1609 a Morris dance was held to entertain the punters at the Hereford races in the heart of cider country. The twelve men who danced had a total age of 1,200 years!

A delicious but simple dish of cod fillet cooked in dry cider.

SERVES 4

3 tbsp oil
1 onion, peeled and finely chopped
2 cloves garlic, peeled and crushed
2 leeks, trimmed, thinly sliced and washed
1½lb/700g cod fillet, skinned and in chunks
¼pt/150ml fish stock
1 wine glass dry cider
3 tbsp double cream
1 tbsp freshly snipped chives
salt and freshly ground black pepper

Heat oil in a pan and fry onion and garlic until soft but not browned. Add leeks and stir around until softened. Add cod chunks and cook for a further minute, stirring. Pour over stock and cider and bring to the boil. Lower heat then simmer until fish is cooked through, about 15 minutes. Stir in cream and chives, and season with salt and freshly ground black pepper. Pile into a warmed dish to serve.

DRINKS: Dry cider or a dry white wine like white Rioja or Soave.

Country Rabbit in Cider

In the seventeenth century, when cider was a popular drink in England, it was widely thought to have medicinal powers. In his interesting book, The History and Virtues of Cyder, *the author R. K. French says trial and error established cider had two major effects. When made with certain equipment, it gave the drinker a nasty dose of lead poisoning. When taken in cask on long sea voyages, it was quite a successful antidote to scurvy. It was also thought to be useful in warding off melancholy.*

Little danger of today's 'sanitised for your protection' cider having anything to do with the first two, though it may, I suspect, be able to make you more melancholic.

This rustic recipe harks back to the country origins of real cider.

SERVES 4

4 tbsp oil
4 rashers back bacon, rinded and chopped
1 onion, peeled and finely chopped
2 cloves garlic, peeled and crushed
1 rabbit, in 8 joints
seasoned flour
1 tsp English mustard
¼pt/150ml chicken stock

2 wine glasses dry cider
2 sprigs fresh thyme, chopped
1 tbsp finely chopped fresh parsley
2 tbsp double cream
salt and freshly ground black pepper
extra chopped parsley for decoration

Heat 1 tbsp oil in a pan and fry bacon crisp. Transfer to an ovenproof casserole. Add onion and garlic to pan with another 2 tbsp oil and fry until softened but not brown. Place in casserole with bacon. Dip rabbit in seasoned flour and shake off excess. Add remaining 1 tbsp oil to frying pan and fry rabbit joints to seal and brown. Add to casserole. Stir in mustard. Pour over stock and cider and bring to the boil. Add thyme and parsley, cover and place in the preheated oven at Gas 4/350°F/180°C for 1½ hours or until rabbit is tender.

Remove from oven. Lift out rabbit into a serving dish and keep warm. Place casserole over low heat. Bubble until slightly reduced. Stir in cream and season with salt and freshly ground black pepper. Pour over rabbit in serving dish and decorate with extra chopped parsley.

WINE: This dish needs a white wine with some guts, so I would go for a decent Californian or Australian Chardonnay.

Pot-Roast of Chicken with Cider

The making of cider is the preserve of the Normandy region of France and the south of England, particularly the county of Somerset. It was the early Celts who introduced apple trees to both regions. Cider played an important part in the rites of the Druids, and it would be nice to think that after the summer solstice at Stonehenge, one Druid would turn to another and say 'Now that's over for another year, let's go and get ratted on cider.'

Cider is widely available, and inexpensive, but in the 'industrial' version, which bears little resemblance to the real thing. Unfortunately you have to live in or near a cider-producing region to get hold of the real stuff. Well, perhaps not unfortunately, because real cider can be quite more-ish, with recriminations the morning after.

This recipe is dead easy to make, and delicious.

SERVES 4

3 tbsp oil	3¹/₂lb/1.6kg oven-ready
1 onion, peeled and finely	corn-fed chicken
chopped	¹/₄pt/150ml chicken stock
2 cloves garlic, peeled and	¹/₄pt/150ml dry cider
crushed	1 tbsp freshly snipped chives
2 leeks, trimmed, washed	1 tbsp finely chopped fresh
and finely sliced	parsley
2 carrots, peeled and	salt and freshly ground black
chopped	pepper

Heat oil in a pan and fry onion and garlic until soft but not browned. Remove with a slotted spoon and transfer to a flameproof, ovenproof casserole. Add leeks and carrots to frying pan and toss around for a couple of minutes. Add to casserole.

Place chicken in frying pan and brown on all sides over high heat. Sit on top of vegetables in casserole, breast up. Pour over stock and cider. Add chives and parsley. Season with salt and freshly ground black pepper. Bring to the boil, then cover and place in the preheated oven at Gas 5/375°F/190°C for 1¹/₂ hours or until chicken is cooked through. Check seasoning and serve straight from the pot.

WINE: Unfortunately the presence of cider makes this difficult. You can drink cider with the dish, but if you prefer a white wine, I would go for something simple like Frascati, Soave or Verdicchio. If the guests are a bit more posh, select a dry white Graves.

Somerset Pork
with Scrumpy
and Apples

I have never found very much merit in the drinking of cider, an aversion which I think stems back to an incident in scrumpy cider country in the west of England. I wanted to see a real scrumpy producer and a friend took me to a nearby farm. There a large man with a nose that would have done Rudolph the Red-Nosed Reindeer proud, took us into his barn. There was a collection of ancient casks from which he took generous samples. After an hour or more of this, and by now feeling more than a little frivolous, I asked the farmer how he knew when a particular cask of scrumpy was ready for drinking.

Looking me straight in the eye he replied, 'Ah, I take the lid off and drop in a live rat. If the bugger gets out alive I know that cask is not yet ready for drinking.'

Since then I have confined my acquaintance with cider to its use in the kitchen.

This excellent dish will impress the most hardened mother-in-law.

SERVES 4

3 tbsp oil
3lb/1.4kg loin of pork, boned and rolled
1 onion, peeled and finely chopped
2 cloves garlic, peeled and crushed

12 shallots, peeled
1/4pt/150ml scrumpy or dry cider
1/4pt/150ml stock
salt and freshly ground black pepper

164

2 Cox's Orange Pippins,   4oz/100g button
  cored and in chunks   mushrooms, wiped
1oz/25g butter   2 tsp herb mustard

Heat 1 tbsp oil in a pan and fry pork joint all over to seal
and brown. Lift out and transfer to an ovenproof dish.
Gently fry onion and garlic in remaining oil until softened. Strew around pork. Brown shallots in frying pan
and add these too. Pour scrumpy and stock into frying
pan and stir to scrape up cooking juices. Bring to the boil
and pour over pork. Season and cover with foil. Cook in
the preheated oven at Gas 4/350°F/180°C for 2 hours, or
until pork is tender.

Meanwhile, brown apples in melted butter in a pan.
Add these with mushrooms to pork about 20 minutes
before end of cooking time. Remove foil at this stage
so the meat can brown. When the meat is cooked,
strain juices into a pan and reduce slightly by bubbling
rapidly. Stir in mustard and season with salt and
freshly ground black pepper. Pour over pork and serve
immediately.

WINE: Go for a decent New World Chardonnay.

Cider Cake

In the old days, there used to be hundreds of different varieties of apples used to make cider. The modern apple-grower has narrowed the choice to what are called 'bittersweets' in that they combine the low tannins and sweet flavour with high acidity in the one fruit. This means the cider-maker does not have to 'blend' the juices of the fruits of different varieties to get a balanced flavour.

The preferred bittersweets have some funny names like Brown Stout and Tom Putt. Dabinett, Yarlington Mill, White Beech and Ball's Bitter Sweet are other popular varieties.

Use cider to make this unusual cake for when your mother is coming for afternoon tea.

Serves 6

8oz/225g peeled, cored and
   roughly chopped Bramley
   apples (weighed after
   preparing)
squeeze lemon juice
8oz/225g plain flour
1¹/₂tsp baking powder

pinch salt
4oz/100g unsalted butter
1 tbsp cider
4oz/100g caster sugar
grated zest of 1 lemon
2 eggs

For the glaze
3 tbsp cider

2 tbsp caster sugar

Place chopped apple in a bowl and squeeze over lemon juice. Reserve. Sift flour, baking powder and salt together into a large bowl. Rub in the butter to bread-crumb stage. Add apple, and cider, sugar and lemon zest.

Beat eggs then stir into the mix to make a firm dough. Pack this mixture into a buttered and lined loose-bottomed 7in/18cm cake tin. Smooth over surface. Bake in the preheated oven at Gas 4/350°F/180°C for 50 minutes or until cake is risen and firm. Test with a skewer – if it comes out clean, the cake is cooked.

Meanwhile, mix cider and sugar for the glaze. When the cake is ready, remove from oven and pour glaze over while the cake is still hot. Cool in the tin, then turn out on to a wire rack.

WINE: A glass of Malmsey Madeira.

CHAPTER 9

Whisky

Drunken Haggis

The first time I encountered haggis I was convinced I would not like it, I had heard too much about it. In fact, I loved it, and have since eaten haggis whenever I could. It became a particular pleasure when staying at a good Scottish hotel, where most of the guests were from overseas, to order haggis and watch their horrified looks as I squaffed down a large plateful of what they must have thought was the worst kind of offal.

Back in Australia, haggis is a bit thin on the ground, so I have learnt to make my own — and you don't need a sheep's stomach. Here is how you do it — but if you are serving it to others, it is wise to check that they will actually eat the stuff.

A completely un-authentic version of haggis, this is cooked in an earthenware casserole, and liberally spiked with whisky. Haggis is traditionally served with neeps and tatties. Tatties are, well, tatties. But neeps are not as is commonly thought, turnips. In fact, in Scotland they are swedes mashed with copious amounts of butter and pepper.

SERVES 6

8oz/225g oatmeal

1lb/450g lamb's liver, trimmed of tubes and sliced

1 Spanish onion, peeled and roughly chopped

1½pt/850ml beef stock

2 tbsp oil

1½lb/700g best lean mince

4oz/100g minced beef suet

1 tsp each cayenne pepper, freshly grated nutmeg and mace

1 tsp fresh thyme leaves, finely chopped

1 tbsp finely chopped fresh parsley

salt and freshly ground black   *3 tbsp whisky*
   pepper

Toast oatmeal under the grill until light brown. Reserve. Put the liver and onion in a pan with stock and bring to the boil. Turn down and simmer for 30 minutes. Drain liver and onions and reserve stock.

Heat oil in a heavy-based pan and fry mince in batches until browned. Place mince and oatmeal in a bowl. Coarsely chop liver and onions and add this with suet, cayenne, nutmeg, mace, thyme and parsley. Stir in enough reserved liver stock to make a soft, but not wet mixture. Season with salt and lots of freshly ground black pepper.

Pack into an earthenware ovenproof dish, cover with foil and cook in the preheated oven at Gas 3/325°F/160°C for 1 hour. Remove foil and pour in whisky. Cook at Gas 5/375°F/190°C for 10 minutes to brown the top. Serve with mashed neeps and tatties.

WINE: Stick to malt whisky, though a red Côtes du Rhône will be good too.

Skillet Chook

Of all our feathered friends, the humble chicken is the one I get along with best. Turkey, duck and goose I can handle, but I have a distaste for game birds which dates back to a Christmas in Edinburgh, where an Australian lady friend was living with her husband.

As my birthday is shortly after Christmas and this usually means a week-long drinkathon between Christmas and New Year, she thought she would give me a treat. She bought four plump grouse and hung them out of the window of her apartment. When the evening came to roast them, she reeled them in as we were all sitting in the kitchen having a drink. All we could see were four lumps of flesh, crawling with maggots.

Then there is quail. I never can understand why people order these midget birds then spend the next half an hour trying to get two mouthfuls of food off them. So a plump, free-range chicken it is for me.

A quick chicken dish, flash-cooked with mushrooms and tomatoes in a skillet.

SERVES 4

2 tbsp oil
1 onion, peeled and sliced
2 cloves garlic, peeled and
   crushed
4 rashers streaky bacon,
   rinded and chopped
1oz/25g butter

4 chicken breast fillets, in
   thick slices
salt and freshly ground black
   pepper
4oz/100g small button
   mushrooms, wiped and
   trimmed

173

4 small tomatoes, quartered
2 tbsp whisky
1 wine glass dry white wine

1 tbsp finely chopped fresh
parsley for decoration

Heat oil in a skillet and fry onion and garlic until soft but
not brown. Remove with a slotted spoon and reserve.
Add bacon to the pan and cook until browned. Add
butter and melt it, then add chicken pieces and toss all
over to brown. Season with salt and freshly ground black
pepper. Add mushrooms and tomatoes to the pan and
cook for a few minutes more. Add whisky and wine and
continue cooking until chicken is tender. Sprinkle with
chopped parsley before serving in the skillet, with sau-
téed potatoes on the side.

WINE: This needs a meaty white like a white
Châteauneuf-du-Pape or a richer Australian or Californian Chardonnay.

Whisky McCurtin

I was once invited to lunch at the offices of White Horse Whisky, which were then above MI5 or MI6, I cannot remember which, across the road from where Langan's Brasserie now stands. Peter, the host, then had an Australian girlfriend and I think he wanted a bit of insider information on how an Australian lassie should be handled.

Peter and I were having a dram when the other guest arrived, Wallace Milroy, distinguished writer on whisky and a legendary malt whisky drinker. I had not met Wallace before, and we subsequently became good friends. Peter asked Wallace what he would have, to which Wallace replied his usual.

Peter went to the cabinet and brought out one of those straight-sided British beer glasses that hold a pint and filled it with Lagavulin, the peaty malt from Islay. I could not believe my eyes. I began to have serious doubts about the rest of the day.

Wallace sipped away as we chatted and soon the glass was empty. Peter suggested we move on to lunch, which, given the circumstances, I heartily agreed with. I later discovered they were teasing me. The day turned out to be fine, for like many others, the two were committed whisky drinkers and just could not handle wine.

This recipe needs some good malt whisky, but fortunately not in the quantity Wallace is used to.

SERVES 4

2 tbsp oil
1oz/25g butter

1 large Spanish onion,
    peeled and thinly sliced

1 tbsp green peppercorns,
  finely chopped
4 fillet steaks
4 tbsp whisky, preferably
  malt

$^1/_2$pt/300ml beef stock
salt and freshly ground black
  pepper

Heat oil and butter in a pan and fry onion over low heat until soft and caramelised. Remove with a slotted spoon, reserve and keep warm.

Press finely chopped peppercorns on to steaks on both sides. Add steaks to pan and cook to preference. Pour over whisky and tilt pan to ignite. When the flames have died down, lift steaks out on to a platter. Pour beef stock into pan and stir to scrape up cooking juices. Bring to the boil and reduce by half. Season with salt and freshly ground black pepper if necessary. Top steaks with caramelised onions and pour over sauce before serving.

DRINK: Whisky if you must or a good red.

Irish Whiskey
Bread and Butter Pudding

When I am in one of my favourite cities, San Francisco, I invariably pay a visit to one of my favourite bars, The Washington Square Bar & Grill. The Washbag, as it is known to its regulars and any taxi-driver who can speak English, is a great place to hang out, and is away from the tourist track.

Co-host is Ed Moose who is a great wine man, to the extent that he will take a bottle off your table to give to another table to taste, and then appear with something different for you to try. Ed also has a passion for baseball, and the bar has a team called the Lapins Sauvages, which travels all over Europe playing matches. It is made up of regulars.

Despite his name, Ed also contrives to be a professional Irishman, and St Patrick's Day at the Washbag is a riot.

Ed's wife, Etta May, is a gifted cook and this recipe is one of hers. No guesses when it is *de rigueur*.

SERVES 6

3oz/75g sultanas	*pinch salt*
1/2 wine glass Irish whiskey	*softened butter for spreading*
2 eggs	*6 slices French bread*
2 egg yolks	*1/2pt/300ml milk*
few drops vanilla essence	*1/4pt/150ml double cream*
3oz/75g caster sugar	*icing sugar for dusting*

Soak sultanas in whiskey for 30 minutes. Beat together eggs, yolks, vanilla, sugar and salt. Reserve. Butter French bread slices and arrange in a large buttered ovenproof dish, in one layer, buttered sides up.

Heat milk and cream until just below boiling point. Whisk on to reserved egg mixture. Strain sultanas, pouring whiskey into custard mix, and scatter them over bread in dish. Strain custard and pour over. Place dish in a roasting tray half filled with water. Bake in the pre-heated oven at Gas 5/375°F/190°C for 30 minutes or until firm. Test with a skewer, and if it comes out clean then the pudding is ready.

Remove from oven and dust with icing sugar. Place under a preheated grill to brown. Serve with thick double cream flavoured with whiskey or a little Irish Mist liqueur.

WINE: An inexpensive sparkling wine, Asti Spumante, or Irish Mist liqueur.

Ginger Fool

If you are in London, it is worth a visit to the premises of Messrs Berry Brothers and Rudd in St James's. One of the oldest wine merchants in the world, their premises are a Pickwickian delight. The other reason for visiting them is to get a bottle or two of their King's Ginger Liqueur. This is not the lower strength green ginger wine, a British speciality, but a serious liqueur based, I think, on whisky. It is one of the very few liqueurs I know that has ginger as the dominant flavour, and it makes a wonderful winter warmer.

This speedy dessert calls for Irish whiskey rather than Scotch, but a dash of King's Ginger Liqueur works well.

SERVES 4

6 ginger biscuits
1pt/600ml whipping cream
3 tbsp Irish whiskey
1 tbsp caster sugar
1 tbsp preserved stem ginger
  in syrup, finely chopped

1 tbsp juice from the jar
sliced preserved stem ginger
  for decoration

Crush biscuits in a food processor – or by placing them in a polythene bag and reducing to crumbs with a rolling pin.

Whisk cream with whiskey and sugar until stiff. Stir in crushed biscuits, preserved stem ginger and ginger juice. Spoon into glasses and chill for an hour. Decorate with more slices of stem ginger.

WINE: Any sweet or sparkling wine.

Whisky Marmalade

On my first-ever visit to Glasgow, a city I came to enjoy very much when it got its act together, I arrived by train at night. The hotel was just around the corner, so I legged it over with my bags, only to discover the door was chained with chains that could have held a small cargo liner at anchor.

However, there was a light at the end of the hallway so I started to rattle them, while keeping an anxious eye on some rather unsavoury characters who were keeping an eye on me. Eventually the night clerk arrived, unshackled the door and let me in.

I had planned to go out for a meal and a few beers. The clerk informed me that it would be unwise, as it would be unlikely that I would return in the same condition as when I left. But there was a bar and a disco in the basement. When I adjourned there I found about a dozen commercial travellers morosely drinking whisky, while the disc jockey blasted out rubbish music. Why I do not know, as there was not a woman in sight to dance with. The next morning I had a bit of a sore head and could not face the marmalade.

This is a relaxing way to fill in some spare time and some tokens of appreciation for people who invite you to dinner.

FILLS 3 × 1LB/500G JARS APPROX

3lb/1.4kg Seville oranges
juice of 1 lemon
2¹/₂pts/1.5 litres water

3lb/1.4kg preserving sugar
3fl oz/75ml whisky

Wash and dry oranges and thinly pare away the peel,

leaving behind the pith. Cut peel into thin shreds and reserve.

Quarter peeled oranges and remove pith and pips with a sharp knife. A serrated one works best with the pith. Tie these up in a piece of muslin. Place in a preserving pan with roughly chopped orange flesh, lemon juice and water. Bring to the boil then turn down to simmer for about 1 hour, or until water is reduced by half.

Remove muslin bag, squeeze out well, then discard. Add sugar and stir until completely dissolved. Bring back to the boil and continue boiling rapidly until setting point is reached – about 20 minutes. Test this by spooning a little on to a saucer – it should wrinkle when pushed gently with a finger. Add whisky and boil for another 5 minutes. Cool slightly then pack into warmed sterile jars. Cover and seal.

CHAPTER 10

Gin, Rum and Vodka

Plymouth Soup

Of all the major spirits, the one with which I have the greatest affinity is gin. I think this goes back to my youth when my parents were regular gin and tonic drinkers until, for some unexplained reason, they switched to brandy and soda.

There was always a bottle of Beefeater around, but when I got to London, I discovered there was more to gin than Beefeater, and discovered the delights of what I consider to be the two best gins in the world, Plymouth and Bombay.

Plymouth is made in the English town of the same name in the Black Friars distillery. Parts of the distillery are bits of a former monastery, built in 1425 by a Dominican order of Black Friars. Their refectory, with a curved timber ceiling like the upturned hull of a man o'war, still stands and is classified as an ancient monument. It was here the Pilgrim Fathers spent their last night in 1620, before sailing off to America. Bombay, as any New York barman will tell you, is the only gin to use in a Dry Martini.

Some say gin has medicinal qualities. All I can say is that a couple of stiff gin and tonics have saved my bacon on more than one occasion.

An easy-to-make and richly flavoured carrot soup spiked with gin. Another bacon-saver.

SERVES 4

2 tbsp oil
1 onion, peeled and roughly
   chopped

2 cloves garlic, peeled and
   crushed
4 carrots, peeled and chopped

1 potato, peeled and in
  chunks
1 tbsp tomato purée
1 tbsp fresh parsley, finely
  chopped
salt and freshly ground black
  pepper

1³/4pts/1 litre chicken or
  vegetable stock
3 tbsp gin, or to taste
tiny croûtons
extra chopped fresh parsley
  for decoration

Heat oil in a pan and fry onion and garlic over gentle heat until softened. Add carrots, potato, tomato purée and parsley, and cook for about 10 minutes, still over low heat, to bring the flavour out of the carrot. Season. Pour over stock and bring to the boil. Turn down to simmer and cook, covered, for about 25 minutes, or until vegetables are tender. Taste and adjust seasoning if necessary. This soup can take a lot of pepper. Whizz smooth in a blender or processor.

Return to a clean pan, add gin, and bring back to bubbling. Serve sprinkled with tiny croûtons and extra fresh chopped parsley.

WINE: A lightly chilled fino sherry.

The Perfect Bloody Mary

The first Bloody Mary was fixed by Ferdinand Petiot in 1920. Petiot was the barman at Harry's New York bar in Paris. One of the customers, entertainer Ron Barton, named the original the Bucket of Blood, after a Chicago club he had worked in.

Not much happened until the Americans started to take to vodka in the 1940s, and several new vodka cocktails were invented, including the re-invention of the Bloody Mary.

Use Smirnoff or an English vodka for this, not Polish or Russian which are too strong. This recipe comes from L'Otel, in Kings Cross, Sydney.

MAKES 1

*juice of 1 whole lime, or ½
    lemon, at least 2 tbsp
salt and freshly ground black
    pepper
ice*

*vodka
Tabasco
tomato juice
celery stick stirrer with leaves
    on the top*

Squeeze a little lime or lemon juice into a saucer. Dip the rim of a large glass (500ml/17fl oz) into juice, then into some salt, so it sticks on.

Place 5 ice cubes in the glass. Cover with vodka by ½in/1cm (more or less to preference – this amount is pretty potent). Add lime or lemon juice – lime is best. Shake over three good dashes Tabasco – this is *essential*. Fill to the top with tomato juice. Season with salt and freshly ground black pepper. Stick celery stirrer in. Drink with a straw – seriously – that's right.

Pasta with Bloody Mary Sauce

*There are those days when the body is just a touch fatigued from
the indulgences of the night before. I must admit I have had my
fair share. Lying around moaning about your self-imposed
problem is not the answer. Positive action is needed.*

*The secret is to mix a Perfect Bloody Mary (see page 187)
and drink it while preparing this dish as a late breakfast or
brunch.*

This dish, based on a rich tomato sauce spiked with
Tabasco and vodka, can of course be served at other
times, and makes a wonderful talking point.

SERVES 4

2 tbsp oil
1 onion, peeled and finely
 chopped
2 cloves garlic, peeled and
 crushed
2 sticks celery, chopped
1lb/450g fresh tomatoes,
 peeled, seeded and roughly
 chopped
14oz/400g can chopped
 tomatoes
2 tbsp tomato purée

1 tsp dried oregano
seriously good shake of
 Tabasco, or to taste
juice and zest of 1 lime
salt and freshly ground black
 pepper
2 tbsp vodka
12oz/350g spaghetti
2 tbsp olive oil
freshly grated Parmesan
 cheese for serving

Heat oil in a pan and gently fry onion, garlic and celery
over low heat until softened. Add fresh tomatoes,
canned tomatoes, tomato purée and oregano. Simmer
until sauce is reduced by about a third. Add Tabasco,

188

and lime juice and zest. Then season with salt and freshly ground black pepper. Finally pour in vodka and bring to bubbling.

Meanwhile cook spaghetti in plenty of boiling salted water until just tender. Drain and stir olive oil through. Pile into a huge serving bowl and pour sauce over. Serve with freshly grated Parmesan cheese.

WINE: Valpolicella, Bardolino or Rosso Cònero would be a good foil for this.

Mint and Grapefruit Spritz

This very simple and quick recipe calls for a dash of vodka. Instead of reaching for the Smirnoff, I suggest you put in a little time and try to find a bottle of the Russian Limonnya vodka, a vodka flavoured with lemon rind.

Interestingly, one reason why vodka is such a popular drink with Russians, Poles and others is that in many parts of their countries the winters are so severe, beer or wine would simply freeze at those temperatures, whereas vodka remains liquid.

A refreshing and juicy fruit salad. Use ripe grapefruit.

SERVES 4

2 large ripe sweet grapefruit
1 tbsp mint syrup
3 tbsp vodka

1 tbsp fresh mint, finely
    chopped
mint sprig for decoration

Carefully peel grapefruits, removing all the pith, then cut into segments towards the central core removing all the membranes. Place grapefruit flesh in a glass bowl and pour over mint syrup and vodka. Stir, then leave to infuse for half an hour.

Stir through chopped mint just before serving and decorate with a mint sprig.

DRINK: A good vodka or even a Crème de Menthe to echo the mint flavour of the spritz.

Peaches Baked with Rum

On one occasion, two of us found ourselves overnighting in a rather swish hotel on Sri Lanka, and as I have more than a professional interest in spirits, I was keen to try the local version of arrack. Arrack, or raki, is a spirit often found in the Far East made from molasses, rice, coconut palm juice, the flowers of the mahau plant or of the deciduous butter tree, dates and cashew nuts. If arrack has an affinity it is with white rum.

Anyway we went to the main bar, only to find it closed. The second bar by the pool was also closed. On asking why at the front desk, we were told that it was the night of the full moon. What the hell has that got to do with the price of a drink, I thought. Apparently the local religion forbids the serving of alcohol when there is a full moon. Fortunately, a couple on our tour had lost their luggage – and we were able to swap them some clean clothes for a bottle of Captain Morgan rum.

This dish can be made using the leftovers at the bottom of the rum bottle.

4 large ripe peaches
2 tbsp stale cake crumbs
1 tbsp soft brown sugar

¹/₂tsp ground cinnamon
2 tbsp dark rum

Skin peaches by plunging into boiling water for 2 minutes, draining, then rapidly pulling the skin away using a sharp knife. Halve the peaches, then remove the stones.

Mix cake crumbs with sugar, cinnamon and half the rum and stuff into the cavities in the peaches. Place round side down in an ovenproof dish and sprinkle with remaining rum. Bake in the preheated oven at Gas 5/375°F/190°C for 15 minutes. Serve with cream or ice cream.

WINE: Peaches go well with sweet white table wines like Sauternes or Barsac.

Bananas Guatemala

My father had a full-blown set of Victorian attitudes, including the firmly held belief that men had no role to play in the kitchen, apart from opening the occasional bottle of wine. Then came the day when my mother felt her two sons were old enough to be left in the care of their father. In those days there were no McDonalds, no Chinese takeaways, no delis. The only thing you could buy was fish and chips.

We existed on this, and sandwiches for school. Then one night he stunned us by announcing the serving of dessert. Fortunately he had a fairly relaxed attitude to minors and alcohol, for it turned out to include quite a lot of rum. Where he got it from, I will never know, but it is so simple that even he made a success of it. It has been a favourite of mine ever since.

Fruity, spicy and heady – all the ingredients necessary for a successful dessert.

SERVES 6

6 bananas, peeled and halved
  lengthwise
1/2tsp ground cinnamon
6 tbsp soft brown sugar
6 tbsp lemon juice
6 tbsp hot water

6 tbsp dark rum (if you
  think this is mean, feel
  free to slosh in a bit more
  – I do)
1/2pt/300ml whipped cream

Place halved bananas in an ovenproof dish and sprinkle with cinnamon, sugar, lemon juice and hot water. Cover and place in the preheated oven at Gas 5/375°F/190°C for 20 minutes. Add half the rum and cook for another 10 minutes. Just before serving, heat remaining rum in a pan, pour over the bananas and light it, so blue flames dance across the dish. Serve with whipped cream.

WINE: None required.

Rum Truffle Marquise

I have never had much of an affinity with chocolate, and it has even caused me grief. I was once staying at a lovely, sadly departed, hotel in Cape Town. On my first night, I rather liberally partook of the vinous generosity of my hosts before I finally made it to bed.

When I staggered to the bathroom next morning, I was horrified to see in the mirror that I was covered with a sticky brown substance. When I peeled back the sheets, the bed was covered with the stuff. As I cleaned myself off, I tried to think how I would explain this one away, and reckoned a hefty tip (read bribe) to the housemaid. When I returned to the bedroom, I saw something glinting on the bed. Closer examination revealed silver paper. I had been thrashing around all night in the chocolates which had been kindly left on my pillows.

The hotel manager, who happened to be a friend, issued strict instructions that I was not to be chocolated any more.

With this more-ish recipe, I waive my anti-chocolate feelings.

SERVES 8

3oz/75g plain chocolate,
  melted
6 egg yolks
5oz/150g caster sugar
2 level tbsp instant coffee
  granules, dissolved in 2
  tbsp boiling water

3 tbsp rum
2 tbsp runny honey
5oz/150g unsalted butter,
  softened
3oz/75g cocoa powder
7floz/200ml double cream

FOR DECORATION
2oz/50g plain chocolate

1/4pt/150ml whipping cream

Mix chocolate, egg yolks, sugar, coffee, rum and honey in a large bowl. Beat butter with cocoa powder and stir into chocolate mix. Whip cream stiff and fold in until well blended.

Oil and carefully line a 1lb/450g loaf tin with cling film. Spoon in mix and gently tap base of loaf tin on the work top to knock out any air bubbles. Smooth surface. Chill until set solid, or freeze for a couple of hours to save time.

While marquise is setting, make the chocolate caraque for decoration. Melt chocolate and spread thinly on to a marble board or work surface with a palette knife. Wait until it has almost set. With a sharp cook's knife, holding the blade at 45 degrees to the surface, gently push the blade along the chocolate, so it forms curls as it glides through. Gently place these on a plate and chill.

Turn marquise out on to a pretty platter and peel off film. Whip cream stiff and spoon into a piping bag with a star-shaped nozzle. Pipe swirls of cream along the length of the marquise. Arrange chocolate curls on top. Leave in the fridge until ready to serve.

WINE: An inexpensive Sauternes or Barsac, one of the sweeter German Rieslings or, if you have a very sweet tooth, Muscat de Beaumes de Venise.

CHAPTER 11

Brandy

Farmhouse Country Pâté

My father adored liver, but at home he was in a minority of one.

My first taste of liver was under rather odd circumstances. I was invited by the charming Serge Hocher to visit his famous Château Musar vineyards in Lebanon. One night, Serge took us to dinner with a large group of people at a restaurant in the hills overlooking Beirut. We dined on the terrace. It was all rather bizarre because the Syrians were shelling Beirut, and as we were eating there was a lethal son et lumière *taking place before our very eyes.*

One of the Lebanese treats, or at least Serge said so, was raw liver in a bit of pitta bread with a mint leaf on top. When I declined to taste this, Serge threatened not to open another bottle of his excellent red wine, so I tasted liver for the first time.

This pâté uses pig's liver and belly of pork for a rough-textured terrine you can slice, or spread on crusty bread.

SERVES 10

12oz/350g pig's liver, trimmed of tubes and cut into chunks

8oz/225g belly of pork, boned, rinded and cut into chunks

4oz/100g streaky bacon, rinded and chopped

1 tsp fresh thyme, chopped

1 medium onion, peeled and grated

2 cloves garlic, peeled and crushed

1 egg, beaten

3 tbsp brandy

salt and freshly ground black pepper

3 bay leaves

1 packet aspic (optional)

Mince or process liver – but not too enthusiastically. You don't want a completely smooth paste – unless, of course, you prefer a smoother textured pâté. Transfer to a bowl.

Do the same with the belly of pork, then the bacon. Add these to the bowl with chopped thyme, grated onion and crushed garlic. Next add beaten egg and brandy. Mix all this together until well incorporated. Season with salt and a great deal of freshly ground black pepper. To test if the mix is seasoned enough, heat a little oil in a frying pan and fry a teaspoon of the mix, taste it, then adjust seasoning if necessary.

Place bay leaves in the bottom of a 2lb/900g loaf tin and pack pâté in. Smooth surface. Cover top with foil. Place in a bain-marie and bake in a preheated oven at Gas 3/325°F/160°C for about 1 hour, or until juices run clear. Cool completely before turning out.

Make up aspic according to instructions on the packet. Leave until syrupy and pour over top. Set in the fridge.

WINE: This needs a chunky red from the south of France, preferably something from the Midi.

Steak au Poivre

*I once ordered steak au poivre in a pretty little riverside
restaurant in the Loire Valley. It was nearly a fatal mistake.*

*When the dish arrived the steak was still bleeding inside.
Very politely, I asked if it could be taken back and cooked a
little longer. It soon returned, still seriously raw. I tried to
explain I wanted the steak 'bien cuit'. It was taken back
again.*

*The next minute, the door to the kitchen burst open and the
chef emerged waving a meat cleaver, making it pretty clear it
was me who was going to be 'bien cuit'. In my fractured
French I hastily tried to explain that I came from Australia, and
we like our steak well-cooked there. Suddenly, the chef was all
smiles, said something to my host, and returned to his kitchen.
The host explained that the chef had cooked in Australia for a
few years, and loved the country.*

*Soon the steak returned, this time cooked to perfection —
barbecued.*

Fillet steak pressed with crushed peppercorns and cooked
with brandy and cream. Do ask your friends how they
like their steaks done before you cook this dish.

SERVES 4

2 tbsp black peppercorns
4 fillet steaks
2oz/50g butter
1 tbsp olive oil

3 tbsp brandy
4 tbsp double cream
salt and freshly ground black
  pepper

Crush peppercorns in a pestle and mortar, or if you don't
have one, with a heavy object such as a rolling pin on a

chopping board, with the peppercorns in a bag. Press into both sides of steaks with the fingers.

Heat butter and oil in a pan and over high heat, cook the steaks a couple of minutes each side to seal. Turn down heat – then cook steaks to preference.

Transfer to a hot serving dish and keep warm. Pour brandy into the pan and tilt it so the flames ignite. When the flames have subsided, gradually add cream. Season the sauce with salt and freshly ground black pepper, pour over steaks and serve immediately.

WINE: A decent young claret, Australian or Californian Cabernet Sauvignon, or South African Pinotage.

Steak Diane

Some years ago, an old friend and I were invited to stay the night at a Bordeaux estate, Château Loudenne. We arrived around dinner time to find the château in darkness, but managed to locate the housekeeper. Our host, the late Martin Bamford, had got the dates slightly askew and thought we were arriving the following night. On the phone from Paris, he asked the housekeeper to cook us something to eat, and said that while we were waiting we could get ourselves a drink from a very large and old cupboard in the living room. When we opened the doors, there was a bottle of every product made or distributed by Loudenne's owner, the vast British beverage company, International Distillers and Vintners. That was when I learnt the true meaning of the expression 'like kids in a sweet shop'!

Martin loved his food, and would have enjoyed this dish.

A macho steak dish originating in Australia. Use fillet steak – and plenty of brandy for the flashy flambéeing.

SERVES 4

4 fillet steaks	dash Worcestershire sauce
4oz/100g butter	1 tbsp finely chopped fresh
1 onion, peeled and finely	parsley
chopped	4 tbsp brandy, or to taste
juice and grated zest of ½	salt and freshly ground black
lemon	pepper

Beat steaks with a meat mallet or rolling pin until ¼in/5mm thick.

Melt half the butter in a pan and fry onion over gentle heat until transparent. Remove from pan with a slotted spoon and reserve. Add remaining butter and quickly fry steaks over high heat to preference. Remove and keep warm.

Return onion to pan and stir in lemon juice and zest. Add Worcestershire sauce, parsley and brandy. Tilt pan to ignite brandy, standing back so your eyebrows don't catch fire. When the flames have died down, season with salt and freshly ground black pepper. Place steaks on warmed plates and pour over sauce to serve.

WINE: A decent bottle of claret or Australian Cabernet.

Pork with Calvados

I can only remember being thrown out of one town, and it was not my fault.

The French have a number of wine and spirit brotherhoods, and a small group of us from Britain were invited to be gonged into the brotherhood of Calvados, the French apple brandy. We crossed the Channel to Normandy and found we were booked into a hotel in a small village. That night we arrived at a nearby distillery where the initiation ceremony and dinner were to be held. We were greeted with a mind-boggling array of perfectly horrid cocktails made with Calvados. I mean, who would ever drink a glass of apple brandy and pineapple juice, topped with cream?

The initiation ceremony consisted of each of us having to swig about half a pint of Calvados in one go, and the brandy continued to flow. Around midnight, two or three of us could see serious trouble coming and headed back to the hotel. We let ourselves in and went to bed.

Next morning, all hell broke loose. The proprietor was in a towering rage. We had the only key, and as the others straggled back they kept waking him to let them in. Then he found one of the party had been rather ill in a room he had just finished decorating. The gendarmes arrived as well, wanting to find out who had been in a certain room. It seems the gentleman in question had been caught short in the night, had opened the window and taken a pee. Unfortunately, a gendarme was having a cigarette underneath. We were escorted out of town.

Apples have a great affinity with pork – and so does apple brandy in the sauce of this dish.

SERVES 4

1½lh/700g lean pork, trimmed and cut into chunks
seasoned flour
3 tbsp oil
1 onion, peeled and finely chopped
2 cloves garlic, peeled and crushed
1 tart green dessert apple, peeled, cored and finely diced

1 tsp chopped fresh sage leaves
1 wine glass dry white wine
½pt/300ml pork or chicken stock
salt and freshly ground black pepper
good squeeze lime juice
3 tbsp double cream
3 tbsp Calvados, or to taste

Dip pork chunks in seasoned flour. Heat oil in a pan and fry onion, garlic and apple over gentle heat until soft but not brown. Remove with a slotted spoon and transfer to a flameproof casserole.

Add pork chunks to the pan and toss around over high

heat to brown and seal. Do this in batches – if you crowd the pan, the meat loses the juices because the heat is reduced. Add to the casserole. Add sage. Pour over wine and stock and bring to the boil, then turn down to simmer. Season with salt and freshly ground black pepper and a good squeeze of lime juice. Cook, covered, over low heat for 1 hour or until pork is tender.

Stir in cream and Calvados and bring back to bubbling just before serving.

WINE: A good New World Chardonnay.

Christmas Pudding

Making the Christmas pud is a job for the male of the species, if for no other reason than the male errs on the side of generosity with the alcohol. My brother long claimed to make the best Christmas pud around, so one year I decided to take him on using this recipe.

Australia has draconian laws against importing foodstuffs, so on arrival from London, I went through the red channel and declared the pudding, expecting it to be confiscated. The quarantine officer asked to have a look at it, and when the beast was uncovered had a good sniff. He reeled back and said, 'Christ, mate, if any bug is alive in there, it's welcome to Australia.' My brother now leaves the pud to me.

This pudding is best made at the beginning of the year, and thereafter constantly refreshed with spirituous beverages.

SERVES 8

1 bottle Champagne	2 tbsp finely grated orange
8oz/225g stoned raisins	zest
8oz/225g currants	1 tsp ground cinnamon
6oz/175g fresh brown	1 tsp freshly grated nutmeg
breadcrumbs	1/4 tsp ground cloves
2oz/50g chopped almonds	3 eggs
2oz/50g glacé cherries,	1/4pt/150ml port
quartered	6 tbsp brandy (or rum)
2oz/50g soft brown sugar	

Open Champagne and pour yourself a glass. Drink it. Continue like this through the preparation and cooking until the bottle is finished.

With the exception of the eggs, port and brandy, place all ingredients in a large bowl. Mix together with your hands. In a separate bowl, whisk eggs, port and brandy. Pour over dry ingredients, and mix thoroughly.

Butter a 2pt/1.1 litre pudding basin and turn the mixture into it, leaving a little room at the top for the pudding to rise. Cover the surface of the pudding with a circle of greaseproof paper, and the bowl itself with aluminium foil. Tie the foil around the rim of the basin tightly with string to prevent water getting into the pudding during cooking.

Stand the basin in a large pan, half filled with boiling water. Bring to the boil, then turn down heat to just bubbling. Simmer for 6 hours (even if you increase the ingredients to serve more people). Top up water level during cooking.

Remove from the pan and leave to cool. Remove foil and paper and sprinkle with more brandy. Cover with fresh paper and foil. Store in a cool place.

The longer in advance the pudding is cooked, the better the flavours will marry, but keep refreshing with brandy (or port).

On Christmas Day, cook for a further 2 hours in the same way. Turn pudding out on to a warm serving dish.

Warm a couple of tablespoons of brandy in a ladle, pour over the pudding and light with a match. Take the pudding to the table with the blue flames licking over it. Take a bow to thundcrous applause. Serve with brandy butter.

WINE: Because of the richness of the pudding, a sweet wine will make the combination too cloying. The perfect answer is Champagne or a good sparkling wine, where the acidity will cut through the richness of the pudding.

Brandy Butter

This is the icing on the cake, as they say. However, if you do not have a blender, it takes a long time to make by hand with a whisk. So delegate this task to someone you don't particularly like, such as your mother-in-law.

SERVES 8

1lb/450g unsalted butter   brandy, loads of it
8oz/225g caster sugar

Beat the butter and sugar together until it is pale yellow in colour and fluffy. Start adding the brandy 1 tablespoon at a time only, or the mixture will curdle. Continue until the mix will not absorb any more brandy. Cover with film and chill in the fridge. Serve with the pudding.

Dark Chocolate Brandy Cake

They say the way to a man's heart is through his stomach. Well, the way to a girl's heart is through this chocolate brandy cake. Check she is not a calorie-counter first.

I usually make this cake in the winter, then take the lady for a long walk accompanied by a hip flask of decent Armagnac.

SERVES 8

12oz/350g dark chocolate	*2 tbsp brandy*
6oz/175g unsalted butter	*5 eggs, separated*
6oz/175g caster sugar	*2oz/50g plain flour, sifted*

Melt chocolate in a pan. Add butter and sugar and stir until sugar is melted and all is incorporated. Stir in brandy. Remove from the heat. Beat in egg yolks one at a time.

Whisk the egg whites stiff. Fold half the whites into the chocolate mixture with the flour. Carefully fold in remaining egg whites. Pour the mix into a greased non-stick, loose-bottomed 8in/20cm cake tin. Bake in a

preheated oven at Gas 4/350°F/180°C for around 45 minutes, or until cake is cooked.

DRINKS: Chocolate is a wine killer, so opt for a whisky-based liqueur like Drambuie, or a brandy-based one like Grand Marnier or Armagnac.

Bitter Chocolate Mousses

Chocolate was first introduced into Europe by Christopher Columbus when he brought back cacao beans from Nicaragua on his fourth voyage in 1502. However, no one knew how to treat those cacao beans, so Columbus bombed on this one.

It was the conqueror of Mexico, Hernando Cortés, who first learned about chocolate from the Aztecs, and brought the knowledge back to Spain in 1528. Everybody was so impressed that the Spanish kept the lid on the secret of chocolate for more than a century.

A rich, sensual and irresistible dessert, which uses dark, bitter chocolate.

SERVES 4

6oz/175g dark bitter chocolate	*2 eggs, separated*
	1 tbsp brandy
1 tbsp strong black coffee	*4 coffee beans for decoration*

Break chocolate into squares and place in a bowl with black coffee over a pan of simmering water. Stir until melted and smooth. Leave to cool slightly.

Beat the egg yolks into the mixture. Stir in brandy. Whisk egg whites stiff, then carefully fold into the chocolate mixture. Divide between four small chocolate pots or ramekins. Leave to chill in the fridge. Decorate with coffee beans before serving.

DRINK: Grand Marnier, or a tawny port could be interesting.

Spiced Figs in Armagnac

In the house where I grew up, we had a huge fig tree in the back garden to keep the even bigger mulberry company. It produced so much fruit that there was plenty for us even when the birds had had their share. My father, ever mindful that Australia could introduce Prohibition, used to get some local brandy and marinate the figs in it. I continue this family tradition, though I use Armagnac.

I think my father would have appreciated this alternative use as another way of getting round the Thought Police.

A suitably alcoholic way of preserving figs.

FILLS 1 × 1³/₄PT/1 LITRE JAR

10–12 figs
8oz/225g sugar
¹/₂pt/300ml water
4 cloves

small piece cinnamon stick
Armagnac to cover (about
  ¹/₂pt/300ml)

211

Wash and remove the stems from the figs. Scald them in boiling water. Drain, then prick all over with a needle.

Add sugar to water, then over low heat, stir until sugar has dissolved. Add spices. Bring to the boil and simmer for 5 minutes. Add figs to syrup and simmer gently for 10 minutes.

Using a slotted spoon, lift figs out and transfer to a wide-necked preserving jar. Pour syrup over the figs to come halfway up the sides of the jar. Leave to cool. Fill up the jar with Armagnac. Seal with lid and leave two weeks before eating.

WINE: Try a glass of the Italian liqueur, Amaretto de Saronno, or a sweet white wine like Barsac.

CHAPTER 12

Liqueurs

Melon and Mint Salad

The alcohol addition to this easy recipe is Grand Marnier. This classic French liqueur is remarkable in that there is nothing remarkable about it. No tall tales surround Grand Marnier. The family company of Marnier-Lapostolle was founded in 1827, but the liqueur did not appear until 1880. While the recipe is, of course, a secret, it is basically the flavour of bitter orange peel infused into Cognac.

Grand Marnier brings out the luscious flavour of ripe Galia melon in this simple dessert.

SERVES 4

2 ripe Galia melons
6 tbsp Grand Marnier, or to
  taste
few fresh mint leaves,
  roughly chopped

*icing sugar and mint sprigs
  for decoration*

Halve Galia melons and scrape out seeds. Scoop flesh into balls using a melon-baller, or peel and cut into small chunks. Place in a bowl and pour Grand Marnier over. Add mint leaves and turn gently to mix. Chill for at least an hour or until ready to serve. Arrange melon balls in pretty bowls and pour over any juices. Dredge with icing sugar and decorate with mint sprigs to serve.

WINE: A glass of Grand Marnier or Muscat de Beaumes de Venise.

Salad of Summer Fruits

This fruit salad is one of the best desserts to make to finish a summer meal, or to take on a picnic. Basically, it uses any of the delicate soft fruits that come into the markets in the summer, all of which benefit from a little time in some alcohol.

Fresh soft berries dressed with sweet white wine and Maraschino liqueur.

SERVES 6

1 large punnet strawberries, hulled

1 small punnet fresh raspberries

1 small punnet fresh blackberries

4oz/100g fresh ripe cherries, stoned

4oz/100g white seedless grapes

1 ripe Charentais melon, halved and seeded

1 wine glass sweet white wine

1/2 wine glass Maraschino liqueur

Halve strawberries if they are large, or leave whole if small. Place in a bowl with raspberries, blackberries, cherries and grapes. Peel melon and cut into chunks or scoop out flesh with a melon-baller, and add to bowl.

Pour over white wine and leave to marinate for at least an hour. Add liqueur and turn fruits in the mix. Cover and refrigerate until required. This can be covered and left in the fridge for a couple of hours. Serve with clotted cream.

WINE: A sweet white wine like Sauternes, Barsac or Monbazillac, or any local wine made from grapes affected by the noble rot. Also Asti Spumante or Spanish *cava* sparkling wine.

Amaretto and Nectarine Trifle

Amaretto is one of the liqueurs with a fanciful tale attached to it. According to legend, the painter Bernardino Luini, of the school of Leonardo da Vinci, was commissioned to paint the frescoes for the sanctuary of Santa Maria dei Miracoli in the Italian town of Saronno in 1525. Luini chose as his model for the Madonna a young widow who was running the local inn. In penance for her immorality, the widow steeped apricot kernels and fresh apricots in alcohol to create for Luini a special drink called Amaretto di Saronno, the original recipe for this now famous Italian liqueur.

Whether this actually happened I do not know, but Luini's frescoes do exist. Also while Amaretto is made from apricots, its distinctive taste is of almonds, because of the almond flavour of the apricot kernels.

A super summer dinner-party dessert, with the trifle sponges soaked in this famous Italian liqueur.

SERVES 6

6 trifle sponges
4 tbsp Amaretto liqueur, or
   to taste
4 nectarines
1pt/600ml milk

2 tbsp caster sugar
1 vanilla pod
4 egg yolks
1/4pt/150ml double cream

FOR THE TOPPING
1pt/600ml whipping cream   1 nectarine

Line the base of a large glass trifle bowl with sponges and pour over liqueur. Halve and remove stones from nectarines. Chop and layer over sponges.

Next make the custard. Pour milk into a saucepan and stir in sugar to dissolve over low heat. Add vanilla pod. Bring to just below boiling and remove from heat. Leave to infuse for 15 minutes. Pick out vanilla pod. Whisk egg yolks in bowl and gradually whisk in warm milk. Return to a clean pan and stir over medium heat until thickened. Do not boil. Remove from heat, cover with film to prevent a skin forming and leave to cool. Whip double cream stiff and fold in. Pour over nectarines and sponges in trifle bowl. Chill.

For the topping, whip cream and spoon over custard, reserving a little for decoration. Smooth surface. Spoon remaining cream into a piping bag fitted with a star-shaped nozzle and pipe six swirls on top of trifle. Halve and stone nectarine and cut into six wedges. Sit these on top of swirls. Chill until ready to serve.

WINE: You can serve a glass of Amaretto liqueur, any chilled sweet white wine or, if you can find it, the Hungarian liqueur brandy, Barack Palinka, which is made from apricots.

Blue Ice Cream

Curaçao is one of the liqueurs the Dutch have given the world. It was first made from oranges brought back from the Caribbean island of Curaçao at the beginning of the last century. Oranges were then the rage in Europe, and there were suggestions that oranges were the forbidden fruit. Liqueur producers scrambled to use oranges (the peel, not the juice), and gave us Grand Marnier, Cointreau, Curaçao and the rest. Dutch Huguenots who settled in the Cape also took the recipe with them and created the South African orange-flavoured speciality, Van der Hum.

Most liqueurs made then were coloured, not least because many local liqueurs were made by pâtissiers. Cointreau was the first major liqueur not to be coloured.

Blue Curaçao is mainly used in the mixing of cocktails. Here it finds another role.

The Curaçao colours this ice cream a delicate aquamarine, which belies its orange flavour.

SERVES 4

2 eggs, separated	2 tbsp Blue Curaçao
2 tbsp caster sugar	1/2pt/300ml double cream

Whisk egg yolks and sugar until pale and creamy. Add Curaçao. Whip cream thick and fold in until smoothly incorporated. Whisk egg whites stiff and carefully fold in. Transfer to a freezer tub and freeze. This ice cream can be served straight from the freezer.

WINE: Some more Curaçao.

Crêpes Suzette

There is some confusion over which liqueur you should use in the classic French dessert, Crêpes Suzette. Grand Marnier, Cointreau or brandy are often suggested, but the French gastronomic bible, Larousse, says most restaurateurs have bastardised the dish, and it should be properly made with Curaçao. As all three liqueurs are orange-flavoured, and Grand Marnier also has Cognac in it, I don't think it really matters.

Certainly one of the most delicious and profitable Crêpes Suzette I have had was at a little restaurant in a village outside Oxford. The owners were Belgian and after dinner, offered us Black Label Grand Marnier. I had never heard of it, and as I was writing a book on wine and spirits, was more than interested. They told me it was a special bottling reserved for top French and Belgian restaurants.

Some time later I attended the 150th anniversary party of Grand Marnier, and asked the British sales director if he was going to list Black Label Grand Marnier. He said there was no such thing. I said there was, and bet him the not inconsiderable sum of £50 I was right. The GM managing director was over from France, so we asked him. He of course assured us of its existence, and I collected £50.

This dish is quite easy to cook, and makes a pretty spectacular finale, but your guests have to watch you doing it for the best effect.

4oz/100g plain flour   *1/2pt/300ml milk*
1 egg   *butter for frying*

For the sauce

1oz/25g butter

2oz/50g caster sugar

juice of 2 oranges

juice of 1 lemon

4 tbsp Curaçao

First make the pancakes. Sift flour into a bowl and make a well in the middle. Beat in the egg and a little milk, then stir in the rest of the milk. Melt a little butter in a small pan and pour in enough batter to coat the base of the pan thinly. Swirl it around to distribute it evenly then cook gently until the top bubbles. Flip over and brown the other side. Repeat until all batter is used up. Keep warm.

Melt the butter for the sauce in a large pan and stir in the sugar. Cook over gentle heat until it caramelises. Stir orange and lemon juice into the caramel to make a sauce. Take a pancake and place it in the pan flat. Fold over with a fork to make a semi-circle, then over again. Repeat with remaining pancakes, so they are all in the pan folded up.

Pour over Curaçao and tilt the pan to ignite. Transfer pancakes to a platter, pour over sauce and serve immediately.

Wine: I would opt for a glass or two of sparkling wine.

Raspberry Brûlées

This recipe calls for a dash of raspberry liqueur. For some reason, raspberries have not found much favour with liqueur-producers, and the one you are most likely to find is the clear Eau-de-vie de Framboise from France.

Sensuously glorious little desserts, with raspberries in liqueur underneath the custard and crackly caramel topping.

SERVES 2

1/2pt/300ml double cream *11/2tbsp caster sugar*
1/2 vanilla pod *8 fresh raspberries*
3 egg yolks *2 tbsp raspberry liqueur*

FOR THE TOPPING AND DECORATION
2 tbsp granulated sugar *2 fresh mint sprigs*
2 whole raspberries

Scald cream with vanilla pod and leave for 10 minutes to infuse. Pick out pod. Whisk egg yolks and sugar until slightly thickened. Strain cream on to yolk mix and stir well. Use a double boiler – a bowl over a pan of simmering water – to thicken the custard. Or simply cook in a non-stick pan very slowly over low heat, stirring with a wooden spoon all the time, taking off the heat every now and then, still stirring, until custard thickens enough to coat the back of a spoon. Keep the heat as low as it will go (or the egg will scramble).

Divide raspberries between the base of two ramekins. (Fresh are best – but frozen will do just as well.) Pour over liqueur, then the custard and leave to set. Chill completely.

Sprinkle sugar over the tops and place under a hot grill until sugar has melted and caramelised. Keep your eye on it – it happens in a flash. Leave to cool before serving, topped with the raspberries and mint sprigs.

DRINK: A glass of chilled Framboise.

Cointreau Soufflé

I approached the cooking of my first soufflé with a good deal of trepidation. Soufflés have a reputation for being cantankerous. The friends who were to be on the receiving end of my first soufflé had no doubt mine was going to be a sinker. And I was a little nervous myself. However, when the cooking time was up, I opened the oven door – and lo and behold, a perfectly risen soufflé. I have never been frightened of cooking them since and have discovered they always rise – no matter what you do.

This recipe uses Cointreau, but you can use any liqueur. Grand Marnier, like Cointreau, gives an orange flavour. Use Amaretto for an almondy result, Drambuie for a honey and whisky flavour, or Kahlua for coffee.

SERVES 4

2oz/50g butter
2oz/50g plain flour
1/2pt/300ml milk
2oz/50g caster sugar
4 eggs, separated

4 tbsp Cointreau
grated rind of 1 orange
2 extra egg whites
softened butter and sugar for
    the ramekins

Melt butter in a pan and add flour. Cook 1 minute. Gradually add milk and sugar, stirring continuously to dissolve. Bring to the boil, stirring until thickened. Remove from heat and cool slightly. Beat in egg yolks one by one until glossy. Add Cointreau and orange zest.

Whisk all 6 egg whites stiff in a clean bowl. Gradually fold into the mixture with a metal spoon. Liberally butter the insides of four ramekins, particularly the rim, and sprinkle with sugar to coat.

Spoon soufflé mix into ramekins. Bake in the pre-heated oven at Gas 5/375°F/190°C for 20 minutes, or until well risen and firm to the touch, and top is golden.

WINE: Any sweet white wine or sparkling wine. Or a drop of the same liqueur used in the soufflé. What would be really nice would be a rosé *cava* from Spain.

Atholl Brose with Drambuie

Honey aside, the main flavouring in this classic Scottish dessert is Drambuie, the country's most famous liqueur. The secret recipe for Drambuie is owned by the Mackinnon family who, since they launched the liqueur commercially in 1906, have made a considerable fortune from it.

The recipe was supposedly given to the family by none other than Bonnie Prince Charlie. When the rebellion of the Scottish clans was bloodily put down by the English at Culloden, the prince was forced into hiding. He was given shelter by the Mackinnon of Strathaird, who hid the prince on the island of Skye before helping him escape to exile in France. In gratitude, the prince gave the Mackinnon the recipe for Drambuie, and it has been in the family ever since.

Curious readers may wonder why a prince who is trying to overthrow the English throne is wandering around with a recipe in his sporran. Readers may also speculate what the Mackinnon thought when instead of a whopping great ruby or the like for his services, he received a recipe. 'Och, your Majesty, my wife could really use this,' perhaps?

224

The amounts of honey and liqueur depend on personal preference, so taste as you go to see if you want more or less. Drambuie is malt whisky–based.

SERVES 6

4oz/100g medium oatmeal
3/4pt/450ml thick double
  cream
3 tbsp runny honey (or to
  taste)

4 tbsp Drambuie (or to taste)
extra honey and toasted
  oatmeal for decoration

Toast oatmeal over low heat in a small pan, shaking to prevent burning. Reserve. Whip cream to soft peaks and fold in oatmeal and honey. Stir in Drambuie. Spoon into dishes and top with a drizzle of honey and a sprinkling of toasted oatmeal just before serving.

WINE: Drambuie, malt whisky or dry sparkling wine.

INDEX